THE
LITTLE
HISTORY
OF
NORFOLK

THE
LITTLE
HISTORY
OF
NORFOLK

JOHN A. DAVIES

First published 2020

The History Press
97 St George's Place, Cheltenham,
Gloucestershire, GL50 3QB
www.thehistorypress.co.uk

British Library Cataloguing in Publication Data.
A catalogue record for this book is available from the British Library.

ISBN 978 0 7509 8576 5

Typesetting and origination by The History Press
Printed in Turkey by Imak

CONTENTS

ABOUT THE AUTHOR

John A. Davies was, until December 2018, Chief Curator for Norfolk Museums Service and Director of the 'Norwich Castle: Gateway to Medieval England' project, based at Norwich Castle Museum & Art Gallery. He has worked as an archaeologist in Norfolk since 1984, specialising in the Roman and late prehistoric periods. He undertook his doctoral research into aspects of Roman coinage and has published widely on the subject of coinage from British archaeological sites. Since 1997, in his role as Keeper of Archaeology for Norfolk Museums Service, he has been involved in many archaeological discoveries. His publications include *Land of the Iceni: The Iron Age in Northern East Anglia* (1999), *Venta Icenorum: Caistor St Edmund Roman Town* (2001), *The Land of Boudica: Prehistoric and Roman Norfolk* (2009), *Boudica: Her Life, Times and Legacy* (2009), *The Iron Age in Northern East Anglia: New Work in the Land of the Iceni* (2011), *Castles and the Anglo-Norman World* (2015) and *A History of Norfolk in 100 Objects* (2015). He is a Fellow of the Society of Antiquaries.

ACKNOWLEDGEMENTS

This work owes a debt to the many authors, historians, archaeologists, archivists, local enthusiasts, metal detectorists and other finders of archaeological objects, who have contributed so much to our understanding of Norfolk's past. I owe a particular debt to colleagues at Norfolk Museums Service throughout my career with whom I have benefitted from discussions about the county's history, natural environment and cultural context. With regard to this publication, I would particularly like to thank Jan Pitman for his invaluable discussions and advice. I would also like to thank my colleague in the Department of Archaeology, Tim Pestell, whose regular discussions and encouragement towards all aspects of my work have been much appreciated. As always, the views expressed here remain the responsibility of the author.

INTRODUCTION

'We do things differently here'

Norfolk, England's easternmost county, is an area of great and still unspoiled natural beauty. Bounded by a long coastline, golden sandy beaches, panoramic skyscapes; its countryside provides a haven for wildlife. It is populated with elegant stately homes and parklands, charming historic market towns and villages, and bejewelled with a wealth of historic buildings, notably its many medieval churches. It possesses an exceptional wealth of archaeological riches that continue to be discovered daily in the open fields of its widespread agricultural land. The county combines a uniquely varied landscape and geology, while strong maritime influences link it with the North Sea world and beyond. Today, its historic role remains largely forgotten beyond the county borders.

This short history will look at the full span of human occupation in the area now defined as the county of Norfolk. Its origin as a political entity is a comparatively recent imposition, dating back some 970 years, with the first documentary mention of the county in the years 1043–45. The county as a unit was thus in use for the purposes of the new administration, with the arrival of the Normans in 1066.

Unlike many counties, Norfolk is well defined geographically, comprising almost an island, with water on all sides. The Wash and the Fens form the western boundary, with the rivers Little Ouse and Waveney in the south and the North Sea in the east and north. This book will look at this geographical area back through deeper history. It will consider the relationship between the people who have inhabited it and the natural landscape, from the arrival of the very first humans to the present day, and just how this interaction has defined Norfolk's role in national events.

It is not possible, nor is it desirable, in a work of this size, to attempt to cover everything of note that has happened in the county. Neither is it intended to provide a full political history. This account is necessarily a selective interpretation of the flow of events and the reasons underlying them. In particular, I wish to reflect Norfolk's relationship with other areas, which was a changeable interaction. At times the county was at the forefront of innovation and experienced episodes of national prominence. At others, it has been more inward-looking, isolated, and less involved with other regions. Norfolk's role has always been influenced by its unique geographical situation.

Throughout this work I would like to view, perhaps define, Norfolk through its geographical position in two ways. Firstly, the role of water, which has sculpted both its landscape and its character. As well as the sea forming its external borders, Norfolk's rivers have acted as foci for settlement, while providing the means for communications and trade. Waterways have also provided natural routeways, guiding people to and from the county. In respect of its underlying significance, I would term Norfolk as a 'waterland'.

The second definition I wish to apply to Norfolk is as a 'borderland', situated on the periphery, both geographically and in relation to events, which may be further qualified as a form of 'edgeland'. Although not adhering to its strict definition, the latter term does in a simple sense describe Norfolk's location on the eastern extremity of England. We shall see how these three terms remain appropriate for the county's interaction with other parts of the country over time.

PERCEPTIONS OF NORFOLK

Noel Coward's famously dismissive description of Norfolk as 'very flat', in his play *Private Lives*, has long fed perceptions of the county as dull and featureless, and a sleepy quiet backwater, belying its truly diverse landscape and the richness of its history. The quiet rural nature of Norfolk in the twenty-first century also disguises its long and busy past. The county was once one of the most heavily populated parts of England. The county town of Norwich was the largest walled town in the country during the Middle Ages; bigger than London and Southwark combined. As the richest provincial city for much of the seventeenth and eighteenth centuries, it was then recognised as England's second city.

Today, Norfolk is often simply characterised in terms of its agricultural role. Although farming and the associated food service industries remain important, the most significant contributors to its economy, in terms of employment, are actually the wholesale and retail trade, together with the rapidly developing tourism sector.

In terms of communications, Norfolk does indeed lag behind other counties. It has no motorway and less than 100 miles of dual carriageway. There is no railway line connecting the east to the west. It takes an hour and a half to cross the county by car and a similar time to reach the next largest city of Cambridge from Norwich, all of which feeds its perception as an out-of-the-way place.

Norfolk's population is also comparatively small, currently numbering approximately 880,000, which is just fourtieth across England's forty-eight counties. Its population density is 165 per sq km, around one third that of Essex or Kent. Norfolk's landscape is classified as 95 per cent rural, although just over half of the people live in urban parts.

A brief word must be said concerning Norfolk's immediate geographical context. It is frequently referred to as being part of East Anglia. This imprecise term can be misleading and may varyingly embrace other eastern counties including Suffolk, Essex, Cambridgeshire and even Lincolnshire. Historically, its more precise definition derives from 'Kingdom of the East Angles', which essentially links just Norfolk and Suffolk.

THE NATURE OF THE EVIDENCE

There are already many written studies covering all aspects of Norfolk's past, including accounts of the towns, villages and landscape that comprise this distinct county, together with biographies of the inhabitants that have forged its history. In this short work, I look to combine the most significant events within a chronological framework and also within a national context. While doing so, I shall emphasise the themes that have been most important in the development of the county, including those relating to agriculture, industry, maritime history and military influences, religion, thought and writing.

Norfolk's identity has continued to be expressed through the arts, which have uniquely reflected its people's beliefs and their views of the world around them. The different forms of media employed have in turn often been influenced by the local landscape, which continues to provide rich inspiration to artists today.

I have sought to include the contributions of people who have lived here, from the earliest humans yet discovered in the whole of Britain, through to the current population. Many of Norfolk's historical figures are well known and require little introduction, while others have left somewhat slighter traces, which are revealed to us through archaeology.

The pattern and nature of occupation throughout the centuries is reflected in many ways through Norfolk's abundant archaeological remains. The daily lives of our ancestors are brought to life through these treasures, with many new discoveries, and our understanding of more distant times is growing rapidly as a result. They provide a prolific source of evidence from which we can interpret local history, with special reference to periods of technological innovation and social change. Norfolk's material remains are especially strong for the Bronze Age, Iron Age, Anglo-Saxon and medieval periods. The richness of this material owes much to the contribution of amateur enthusiasts and especially metal detector users, who have unearthed a profusion of metalwork, pottery and flint finds. What is particularly special about Norfolk is that these discoveries are routinely reported to, and recorded by, professional archaeologists through the county's well-established system of metal detector liaison, which has been in place since the 1970s – long before this was deemed an acceptable practice in other parts of England.

A note of caution must be raised before using this abundant archaeological material to interpret Norfolk's historic importance. There is no question that the soils of

Norfolk appear abnormally rich in archaeological discoveries. Unfortunately, through the profusion of recorded evidence, we are in danger of over-playing the importance of events here. We must always be wary to assess to what extent the number of finds represent genuine historical significance at any stage, and how much they just reflect the efficient reporting and recording of finds from within a rural landscape.

Norfolk is also rich in historic buildings. For the past 2,000 years its inhabitants have been leaving a legacy in the form of stone constructions. Many structures dating back over 1,700 years still survive above ground; particularly those built over the last thousand years. Both secular and religious buildings illustrate the historic past at its different stages. Together, they are able to reveal the character of the people and the societies that created them. The development of buildings over time also reflects art styles, thought and the wider cultural associations of our ancestors. Norfolk is particularly well known for its churches but it is through its secular buildings, including its great castles, that much of the county's past is revealed. All of these great surviving structures are a direct and evocative link to periods throughout our history.

BORDERLAND

Jutting out into the North Sea, the area has always had an international outlook and connections. It is sometimes assumed that the long North Sea coastline has acted as a cultural barrier. Norfolk's history, as we shall explore, shows that it has in fact served as a significant link between populations, with social bonds reaching back millennia. The county's location close to mainland Europe has ensured that it has often been at the forefront of receiving new ideas from abroad and, on occasions, to experience the initial impact of invasions. It has frequently acted as a well-trod route into Britain for both invaders and long-distance travellers. The sea has also provided Norfolk with the means of generating wealth through trading links and direct economic benefits such as fishing.

Norfolk was not always bounded by sea. Britain was once joined to the continent of Europe at this point and the sea lay far off to the north. The coast formed a line running from the current Yorkshire coast to the northern tip of Denmark. The area that is now the North Sea was a fertile plain, populated by vast herds of migrating animals, in the way that the Serengeti plain is inhabited by big game in modern times.

The sea level eventually rose, steadily encroaching upon the land. However, it was not until around 8,000 years ago that the coastline reached approximately its present-day position, leaving Norfolk prominently exposed on the eastern edge of Britain. From about 3,000 until about 1,600 years ago, sea levels rose once again and coastal estuaries and marshes were extensively flooded. Today's rivers were broader and deeper and formed more significant boundaries. After the Roman period, water levels dropped. This recurring cycle has continued, with sea levels rising again before the thirteenth century.

Once again, at the outset of the twenty-first century, the natural process of coastal change is causing devastation for coastal communities and signalling alarm for the resident population on Norfolk's eastern edge. The soft shale and clay of its shoreline are being eroded and moulded at an alarming rate. At the same time, this process is serving to expose fascinating new evidence of former historic landscapes.

THE LANDSCAPE OF NORFOLK

Noel Coward's description of Norfolk as 'very flat' was not in fact at all accurate, as any cyclist in the county will readily testify. In fact, it comprises a complex and diverse landscape, embracing a number of sub-regions that are all very different in appearance, together with a series of inter-locking borderlands where these different regions come together, providing a rich combination of natural resources.

The most influential single aspect of Norfolk's landscape is water, which has always dominated the area. The long and varied coastline contains stretches of dunes, shingle banks and marshes. Sea and rivers have been key to the development of its communications, transport and econ-omy. Nowhere in Norfolk is more than 65km from the sea.

The influence of the coast and of waterways was equally significant in earlier times, way back into prehistory. Ports have been situated at key locations around the coastline for many centuries, as far back as we can trace. They have been the focus of prolific activity and trade that has, in turn, been the source of great wealth. In historical times, major trade routes have linked the area with Scandinavia, Russia, the mainland of northern Europe and the Mediterranean. Commerce has also been generated from coastal fishing.

The county is separated from the midlands to the west by the Fenland basin. The main land connection is to the south through Suffolk. Long deep-seated local rivalries have formed a contrasting type of barrier with the 'South Folk' in that direction. In the north-west the Goodsands comprise an area of rolling upland with fertile soils, good for growing cereals, especially barley and also provides good grazing. In the west of the county is the Greensand belt. These deposits are acidic, free-draining, and are associated with heathland.

The area contains iron-rich strata and produces a form of local building material, known as carrstone.

In the centre of the county, and running through to the south-east, lays a thick covering of boulder clay. This becomes easily waterlogged and has often been avoided for agriculture. In the less-fertile parts, the greatest concentration of ancient woodland can still be found. This region is particularly good for cereal production. The central watershed runs in an arc through the clayland and divides the rivers that flow towards the east coast from those that flow to the Wash, in the west.

To the west of the claylands lies the Breckland, which is a region of undulating heathland, spanning the Norfolk–Suffolk border. It has low rainfall and suffers extreme temperatures, which include warm summers and late frosts. It has light soils, which are marginally productive but with good drainage. The ancient trackway known as the Icknield Way passes through this region.

The Broads are a wetland zone that lies between Norwich and the east coast. They were formed as disused medieval peat workings which flooded with water. Today the Broads are a National Park visited by thousands of holidaymakers each year.

There are 200 square miles of Norfolk Fens. Exploitation of the Fenland has always been dependent on changing sea levels. The northern part, adjacent to the Wash, is covered by marine silt, which was laid down just before the Roman conquest. In the south are the black peat fens.

It is also important to mention a little-known feature thats lies just beyond the North Norfolk coast. Europe's longest chalk reef extends between the sea north of Sheringham Park eastwards through to Cromer. The reef comprises a unique biodiversity habitat, providing home to hundreds of species of fish and plant life. It also provides the clean and nutrient-rich conditions that produce the flavoursome crabs, for which Cromer is famous.

NORFOLK'S FAUNA

Norfolk has a relatively young geology, which means that it lacks evidence for Britain's most ancient fauna, such as dinosaurs. However, the county's sands, gravels clays and peats contain the fossil bones of a large variety of other exotic creatures. The world-famous Cromer Forest Bed, which dates back 1.5 million years, has revealed evidence of giant mammals including four species of mammoth (more than any other part of Britain), giant hippos, rhinoceros and even large sabre-tooth cats.

Norfolk has seen great diversity in the species that have lived here. It is impossible to state just what should be considered to be the native fauna of the area, as this would have differed profoundly, depending on the date in question over the last million years. Through its location as an edgeland and its contacts with the wider world, the area has absorbed waves of immigrant species and been the home of many exotic and diverse creatures, with a series of changing ecosystems over time. Species have included such creatures as elephants, mammoths, lions, hippopotamus, hyaenas, monkeys and giant elk. Animals and plants have adapted to the changing habitats and many others have become extinct. In fact, it has been our ancestors that have been largely responsible for killing off most of the larger land mammals that have lived here.

So, the species considered native to Norfolk have changed with the development of the land, the forces that have moulded it and also through the influence of the humans who have lived here. New animal and plant species have accompanied waves of incoming humans who have arrived to settle through time.

Today, Norfolk is considered to be *the* top county for birdwatching. This has been ascribed to its geographical location on the edge of Britain, jutting into the North Sea, pointing towards Europe and Scandinavia. Many bird species make landfall here, often as stopovers on longer routes, and make use of its diverse range of especially watery habitats.

NATURAL MATERIALS

The appearance of its historic built environment has been governed by the fact that Norfolk suffers from a lack of good building stone. The people who have lived in this part of the country have needed to either adapt other local materials for construction purposes or bring in stone from further afield if they have been wealthy enough. One native form of building stone is flint, which has led to a distinctive appearance to buildings across some parts of the county, where the chalk bedrock has provided an abundance of this material. The flint of Breckland is exceptional in quality and has been used in buildings and as tools for thousands of years.

Other natural building materials include the form of brown sandstone in West Norfolk called carrstone. Ironstone is also found in the west. In Breckland, a yellow-grey form of chalk rubble, known as 'clunch', has been used for construction. Chalk has also been used right across the county. However, the most ubiquitous building material in this rural county has always been timber, which means that so many of its historic buildings have not survived.

The lack of mineral wealth, coupled with the richness of its soils, have made Norfolk more suited to profitable agriculture than to industry. It was for this reason that the county was largely bypassed by the Industrial Revolution.

CLIMATE

Britain's prevailing weather comes from the west and is influenced by the Gulf Stream. Norfolk, situated in the far east, has less exposure to the westerly conditions, winds and rainfall, which means that it is the driest county in England. Nowhere in the county receives more than 27 in of rain each year. Norfolk's unique climate has been another important factor in its agricultural prosperity, being particularly suited to the production of arable crops, which has been the case from very earliest times.

This area is also characterised by occasional very cold winters. Although the county has a predominantly mild climate, its eastern maritime location and low topography can give rise to difficult winters when prevailing conditions switch to the east and biting winds speed in across the North Sea, unstopped by any physical barrier, direct from Russia's Ural Mountains.

WHY STUDY NORFOLK'S HISTORY?

Norfolk's past is not well known on the national stage, despite the amount of historical research it has received. The county has a vivid history that is an integral part of the wider and unfolding national story and deserves to be better understood. As a nation, we continue to learn from our past. It can be said that what happens in the present often has roots deep in our history. Written records and the material culture of our ancestors revealed through archaeology provide us with an insight into the beliefs and actions of previous generations. Historical issues, involving the relationship between belief, religion and the state, have a continuing resonance in the modern world. Such current issues as multiculturalism similarly have echoes in the past that we can learn from.

Norfolk's history has been inextricably entwined in a series of revolutions, of which some have been in the form of ideas and technological developments. Invasions from abroad have been another recurring theme. The study of Norfolk's history shows how successive waves of people and foreign influences can be absorbed and contribute to a cohesive, strong, identity and a stable but progressive society. The new, incoming peoples did not always stay but often moved through to other locations. In such cases, Norfolk's role was often that of a routeway to other parts of Britain.

Norfolk has played a role at all stages throughout the broader history of England. The large amount of research and archaeological attention it has received allows us to determine the periods when it was at the forefront of national developments as well as identifying when it played a more detached, inward-looking, complementary role. But its history throughout is integral to understanding the national story.

It is perhaps ironic that, given its role as a routeway, the county became somewhat isolated during the latter stages of the twentieth century. People have not passed through on the way to other parts of Britain. Coupled with the slowness of communications, its geographical position has meant that, in modern times, it has often been considered a 'dead-end' location. Now, improved road and rail links, coupled with its promotion as a tourist destination, are changing things and in the twenty-first century, Norfolk is regaining a national profile.

This short history has needed to be restricted and selective in its coverage of past events. Inevitably, there have been many omissions. Wherever possible, I have looked to draw on the lives of real people who have lived in the county and shaped our history and to follow events through their contributions.

To follow the relationship between the people, from those who first visited and then settled in this area, with the developing landscape, which they subsequently shaped and moulded over time, is to recognise the forging of the modern Norfolk character. The motto of the University of East Anglia is '*Do Different*'; a strapline that has subsequently been associated with the county of Norfolk as a distinct and special place. In this work we shall investigate to what extent, and on what occasions, Norfolk's people have in fact '*done different*'.

1

THE EARLIEST PEOPLE

The First Million Years

It was close to one million years ago that the first humans, who were distant relatives of today's population, first set foot on the soil of what is now Norfolk. Recent discoveries from the county's north coast have revealed evidence that has dated the arrival of these first people to double the age evidenced anywhere else in Britain. These were explorers; pioneers moving out into unknown parts of the world. They were intent on pushing forward even into the coldest, less hospitable and marginal lands, braving the very harshest climate in search of food, shelter and resources, while at the same time embodying the same spirit of exploration and curiosity that we recognise today.

The earliest humans had evolved in Africa over two million years ago. Their descendants spread outwards, expanding north and west across Europe. It was not until much later, just some 100,000 years ago, that our direct ancestors, modern humans or *Homo sapiens*, evolved in Africa. They too began to move outwards, eventually populating the whole world.

The enormous timespan covered by this initial period in our story, stretching from the arrival of the very first humans until approximately 8000 BC, is called the Palaeolithic. Norfolk contains some unique and internationally significant evidence from this period that throws new light on the human colonisation of Europe.

THE LAND

Britain was physically joined to the continent of Europe at this time. Today's flat Norfolk landscape was once covered by hills and valleys, more similar in appearance to parts of northern Britain today. This was the Ice Age, which lasted between 700,000 and 10,000 years ago. During that time, the world's climate changed dramatically. Not only was the landscape very different in appearance, but it also suffered extreme climatic conditions, often much colder and drier than today. The prevailing cold conditions were occasionally interrupted by warmer periods, when the climate was much more similar to that of today, called interglacials, followed by more extreme phases of intense cold and glaciation. Glacial ice steadily scoured the land, finally leaving it flat as we find it today. Sea levels fell hugely on occasions – by as much as 100m during the times when water became ice. Norfolk was positioned at the edge of the glaciations; partially covered by ice sheets during the Devensian and Wolstonian and completely covered during the Anglian (oldest) phase.

Ice Age Norfolk was the home of huge and exotic creatures. Giant elephants taller than double-decker buses roamed the landscape. They were preyed on by huge cats and, eventually, their carcases were dismembered by scavengers, such as hyaenas, in a scenario we would consider more characteristic of today's African savannah. Less than 10 miles east of Norwich, astonishing evidence has been collected for some very large exotic mammals. A site at Norton Subcourse has revealed fossil skeletons belonging to creatures who lived during a warm period between 750,000 and 500,000 years ago. Fossil bones include those of a giant form of hippopotamus, weighing between 6 and 7 tonnes (compared with a mere 4 tonnes of the modern hippo).

Much of our evidence for these creatures comes from the dark geological deposit known as the Cromer Forest Bed, situated at the base of the cliffs lining the northern East Anglian coast. It is exposed at intervals around the east coast between Weybourne in the north and Kessingland (Suffolk) in the south. Laid down between 1.5 million and 500,000 years ago and now beneath the sands and gravels left by glaciers, it has long been famous for the fossil remains that it contains. Some thirty years ago the most spectacular discovery was made.

In 1990 some enormous bones were exposed, which were later identified as those of a male mammoth who lived between 600,000 and 700,000 years ago. It belonged to the species *Mammuthus trogontherii*, otherwise known as the Steppe Mammoth, which was probably the largest species of mammoth that ever lived. The creature originally stood a huge 4.5m at the shoulder and weighed 10 tons, double the weight of the largest elephant living today. What became known as the West Runton Mammoth is the oldest mammoth skeleton ever to be found in Britain. During its lifetime, much of the Norfolk landscape probably looked similar to today's Norfolk Broads.

When first discovered, the West Runton Mammoth was thought to have come from a time long before the first humans reached Britain. Just a decade later, this changed as further significant discoveries were made just 30km along the coast at Happisburgh.

THE FIRST PEOPLE

Erosion continues to accelerate along the length of coast between Great Yarmouth and Cromer, making this the fastest retreating stretch of coastline in Europe today. Storms in early 2018 left hundreds of coastal homes threatened with destruction, most recently in the vicinity of Hemsby. One of the worst-affected beaches is at Happisburgh, where the cliffs have been eroded into an embayment, currently reaching inland some 100m from the original cliff line. This location had once been part of the floodplain of an ancient river. Until less than 20 years ago it was thought that the earliest humans in Britain arrived in the south of England 500,000 years ago. Discoveries at Happisburgh have doubled the known duration of human occupation in Britain.

It was in 2013 that a remarkable discovery was made. Following winter and spring storms, Happisburgh's foreshore revealed a series of impressions in the estuarine muds. Detailed study showed that these hollows were fossil footprints. They had been left behind by a group of at least five people, perhaps a family group, which included an adult male, females and possibly adolescents and children. These footprints are evidence of the very first people to arrive in what is now Norfolk some 950,000 years ago. Their arrival can be associated with the landscape and the creatures it supported, on which they were dependent.

These early people were from a species known as *Homo antecessor*, an early form of human who would have looked fairly similar to us. They had large brains and used a basic range of stone tools. They would have feared the abundant predators and rarely hunted the really big game around them. They mainly hunted smaller creatures and gathered plants.

Happisburgh was situated on a natural routeway north as people spread further and further out across Europe. Ongoing research there has shown how humans were exploiting this area, as they moved from a familiar Mediterranean habitat into northern forested areas and coping with lower winter temperatures. The discovery was made here because the location is at a point where geological deposits of that date coincide with both coastal erosion and an area of ongoing archaeological scrutiny. But early human exploitation need not be unique to this specific area. Other finds of similar antiquity may yet be found elsewhere in Norfolk and possibly elsewhere in Britain.

These findings have profound implications for our understanding of early human behaviour. We now know that the early humans were able to adapt, survive, and were prepared to colonise areas of extreme climatic conditions, following the first human dispersal out of Africa. Norfolk may once again be portrayed as a borderland, situated on the periphery of the habitable world at that time.

Another pre-modern form of early human known to have inhabited Norfolk was *Homo heidelbergensis*. Evidence for this form of early human has again been discovered at Happisburgh, dating from around half a million years ago, through the presence of their flint tools and cut animal bones. The discovery, which was made as recently as the year 2000, can again be attributed to Norfolk's rapidly eroding eastern coastline.

NEANDERTHALS IN NORFOLK

Although humans had been present at these very early times, their occupation of Britain was not continuous. On occasions, this country became too cold to sustain human life. It was deserted for a huge expanse of time between 180,000 and 60,000 years ago before humans, in the form of Neanderthals (*Homo Neanderthalis*), finally returned to Britain. A site at Lynford, near Thetford, has provided evidence for the first human presence in Britain after an absence of 120,000 years. This location would, once again, have been on the very edgeland of habitable land as conditions gradually became warmer.

Lynford is situated in Thetford Forest, and has a group of gravel pits located on the south bank of the River Wissey, where gravel extraction initially revealed the remains of mammoths. Subsequent archaeological investigation found evidence of early human activity in direct association with the mammoth bones, in the form of beautiful fresh-looking black flint handaxes within the same layer of sediment. Significantly, these axes were of the 'bout coupé' form, which were the type of tool used by Neanderthals.

The Lynford site has been dated to between 67,000 and 64,000 years ago, approximately 30,000 years before the arrival of modern humans. The Neanderthals had visited an area of stagnant water surrounded by marshes, next to a large river where both game animals and their predators had come to drink. Reindeer, bison, horse and woolly rhinoceros were accompanied by brown bear and spotted hyaena at the location. A range of human tools was discovered, including some forty-five bout coupé handaxes.

The remains of at least nine woolly mammoths were recovered, making this the only recorded mammoth butchery site known in Britain. It is uncertain whether Lynford's Neanderthals were hunters of the large game animals or merely scavengers of the meat from dead animals. In either event, it is clear that they used their flint tools to remove joints from the mammoth carcases.

THE FIRST MODERN HUMANS

The new species *Homo sapiens* evolved in Africa. It was around 40,000 years ago that these modern humans started to reach Britain, with Norfolk being one of the first locations they came to. *Homo sapiens* are social creatures and these early ancestors lived in family groups or small bands. They developed a more sophisticated language, which facilitated communication with other groups and enabled the benefits of cooperation. They forged bonds with other groups and could expand the group when needed, perhaps for hunting big game or at times of crisis. These early people foraged both for food and for knowledge and clearly had a deep understanding of their surroundings. With *Homo sapiens* came a technological revolution that saw the invention of boats, oil lamps, bows and arrows, and needles. The first art can also be dated to this time.

Now, in addition to the deposits at Happisburgh that have revealed the presence of two species of early *hominin* – *Homo heidelbergensis* and the earlier *Homo antecessor* – the addition of Neanderthals and modern humans, *Homo sapiens*, make Norfolk unique within Britain by having evidence for four species of humans.

THE DISCOVERY OF A WIDER LANDSCAPE

The landscape of Ice Age Norfolk would have been completely unrecognisable to us. Britain was still part of the European landmass, the North Sea was still far away, and small freshwater streams flowed across the great plain of Doggerland that joined Norfolk to the mainland of Europe. One of the most enthralling archaeological projects in recent years has been the mapping of this massive submerged landscape, which is larger than the area of the United Kingdom. Archaeological evidence has been found to show that people were living on the plain and moving across it. It was a discovery on the Leman and Ower Banks in the North Sea, some 40km beyond today's north Norfolk coast, which played a key role in the rediscovery of this sunken landscape.

In 1931 a trawler fishing beyond Cromer dredged up a block of peat from the seabed that contained a beautiful, polished, barbed harpoon or spearhead, which had been made from red deer antler. This magnificent item had been thrown, or perhaps dropped, by a prehistoric hunter. The peat around it had been formed in freshwater conditions, proving that this location had once been inland from the sea. Radiocarbon dating showed that this had been formed around 9800 BC and that the spearhead had been used towards the end of the last Ice Age. This discovery proved that a substantial area of dry land, on the edgeland of what is now Britain, had formed a land bridge with other parts of Europe. Significantly, it also served to focus research into exploration of this lost landscape and, ultimately, the concept of climate change, which is of critical interest today.

The final effects of the ice were coming to an end around 13000 BC. The climate and environment of Britain had begun to change. As conditions became milder, human populations moved north into the area of Norfolk in increasing numbers, following herds of game. These people who arrived as hunters were presented with new opportunities for subsistence and other new challenges as they adapted to new conditions following the end of the age of ice.

2

BRITAIN BECOMES
AN ISLAND

8000 BC–AD 43

The period from around 8000 BC to AD 43 embraced some of the most significant developments in the history of humankind in Britain, involving episodes of revolution and invasion. The period starts with the end of the Ice Age and the occupation of the area by an early indigenous hunter-gatherer population, continuing through the first Agricultural Revolution and the arrival of domesticated plants and animals. The impact of the introduction of farming was to influence all subsequent human development, paving the way for the first settled communities and changing and shaping the way of life of all people through to the present day.

This new and largely peaceful existence was suddenly shattered in a period of catastrophic change as new settlers from mainland Europe rapidly replaced the native farming population. These influential events were not restricted to Norfolk, but the area's geographical location on the exposed east coast ensured that it was in the vanguard to receive the initial impact.

The new settlers introduced the first use of metals to Britain. As time progressed, we later see the coming together of ever larger groups of people, eventually forming into regional tribes. The later years of this period witness the first contacts with the world of Rome.

AFTER THE ICE: THE MESOLITHIC PERIOD

The period from about 8000 BC is known as the Mesolithic, or more popularly the 'Middle Stone Age'. The final throes of the Ice Age saw the last northern ice sheets continue to melt and sea levels rose by between 23mm and 33mm each year. The diminishing land bridge became wet and marshy and it became increasingly hazardous for people to cross. The plain of Doggerland steadily became covered by the North Sea. The relatively large population that had been drawn there by its abundant wildlife and natural resources now needed to move inland, in both directions, as Britain became cut off. Norfolk had become a borderland.

By about 6500 BC, Doggerland had been fully submerged. Britain had become an island and the coastline of Norfolk was broadly in the position that it is today. A coast of beaches, marshes and mudflats formed and provided a rich area for hunting, fishing and gaming. In the far east, water separated the 'uplands' of Flegg and Lothingland, either side of which is Breydon Water, just inland from Great Yarmouth. The land where the town now stands was under water and lakes formed further inland. From this point onwards, cultural development began to develop differently on either side of the North Sea, although ties remained between the populations.

An increase in air temperature meant that the area could now be colonised by plants. Forest spread right across the Norfolk landscape. The open steppe–tundra of the Ice Age gave way to woodland of first birch, then pine, and finally broad-leaf forest. The predominant trees were oak, elm, hazel, lime, ash and maple. Animal species were also changing with the developing climatic conditions.

People and animals steadily returned from further south as the conditions improved. The area of Norfolk became occupied by small groups of mobile hunters and gatherers, who exploited the abundant wildlife that was all around them in the woodlands, marshes, sea and rivers. The homes of these people were temporary structures constructed from trees, branches and wooden stakes. People also made good use of organic material resources such as wood and reeds to make tools and utensils for everyday use. They were a society of skilled people who worked wood and flint to a very high standard. They constructed logboats, which were paddled along Norfolk's rivers and streams, and made bows, spears and harpoons for hunting. Fishing was assisted by the use of nets and fish traps.

There is little surviving evidence for Mesolithic settlements. Most comes in the form of their flint tools, which are most often found on sandy soils next to rivers. One of the richest deposits is at Kelling Heath, close to today's north coast, situated on a high position above Cromer Ridge, where people were making and repairing hunting tools such as spears and arrows. This location provided hunters with a magnificent view for miles distant across the great forested Doggerland plain to the north, in the years before it flooded. From here they could watch the migrating herds of deer and other large mammals, as well as passing bands of other people, for many miles distant.

They would then foray out across the plain from their vantage point.

THE FIRST FARMERS

The Mesolithic was succeeded by the period known as the Neolithic, or 'New Stone Age'. The most significant change was the transition from a hunter-gatherer lifestyle to one that was based on farming. Neolithic settlements are found in East Anglia from about 5000–4000 BC.

The people living around the east coast of Britain continued to have strong cultural ties with the population of the near continent, based on relationships stretching back to before the flooding of Doggerland. They remained in contact with their counterparts in the Low Countries and northern France. As new ideas reached those parts of northern Europe there was then little delay in their reaching eastern Britain. In this way, communities living in the area of Norfolk were some of the first people in Britain to adopt the new farming lifestyle, literally creating the roots of Norfolk's agricultural prosperity that have lasted to the present day.

Domestic wheat and barley, together with the first domesticated animals, were ferried across the North Sea by boat. Early seagoing vessels may have been similar in form to the elaborate Bronze Age boat discovered at Dover in 1992, which was made from sculpted planks that were held together with cleats, wooden wedges and stitches. It had been constructed to withstand the stresses of sea travel and clearly shows that its makers had a sound experience of travel by sea at that early time.

Four species of domestic livestock were initially introduced, which were sheep, goats, cattle and pigs. Sheep and goats were originally natives of the Middle East and had no wild ancestors in Britain. Cattle and pigs did both have wild ancestors, which were the auroch and wild boar. Settlements started to become more permanent and there was less need for people to move around the countryside. At the same time the population began to increase, as a result of the new lifestyle.

Some of the earliest Neolithic settlements in Britain are in East Anglia, at the sites of Shippea Hill in Cambridgeshire and Broome Heath in Norfolk. A gradual adoption of the new farming way of life is suggested by evidence from sites right across Norfolk and in particular from the Fenland in the south-west. At Two Mile Bottom near Thetford, flint microlith tools of the Mesolithic were found alongside Neolithic flint scrapers, together illustrating the development from hunting to farming within a single community.

Neolithic settlement favoured the areas with better drained soils and river valleys. There have been prolific finds of flint tools across Breckland in the south, where the farming population was spreading into this marginal area of woodland. Places of settlement are also indicated by the construction of monuments in the landscape.

Although Norfolk was one of the first parts of Britain to experience and adopt agriculture, it was to be other parts of the country that went on to develop greater prominence. Further west, in Wessex, Neolithic people created an immense ritual landscape, with a wealth of monument construction across Salisbury Plain and Cranborne Chase. The role of water was also significant in the development of sacred landscapes, especially where there was a confluence of river systems. In Norfolk this can be seen in the Tas Valley south of Norwich, where the confluence of the Rivers Yare and Wensum became a focus of settlement and activity in the Neolithic.

Agriculture enabled society to develop in new ways. For the first time, a surplus of food was produced, which enabled non-agricultural workers to be supported, who included other craftsmen and specialists such as flint miners. It was at this time that a mining community was established at Grimes Graves near Thetford in south Norfolk. Here, deep mineshafts were dug in order to reach the best flint for tool-making, coming from the very deepest seams.

Grimes Graves was the largest prehistoric flint mine in Europe. The site was worked for around 500 years, from *c.*2675 BC until *c.*2200 BC. It covers 37 hectares and some 360 individual shafts were sunk up to 15m deep into the ground. Today, the shafts only appear as shallow depressions across the heathland. It has been calculated that some 45 tonnes of flint would have been removed from each shaft, each of which would have been worked by up to twenty miners.

Grimes Graves was a special place that had a status beyond the local region. Flint mines are comparatively rare across Britain and objects made there could have a special importance in Neolithic society. The flint removed from seams deep underground attained an enhanced significance through an association with the special or sacred place. Grimes Graves flint was sought far and wide, not only to make tools but also for its ritual or religious importance.

THE LATER NEOLITHIC

The period of the Later Neolithic can be dated from around 3200 BC. There was an initial rise in sea level, and part of the east coast became covered. Wide river valleys flowed into the Great Estuary where Great Yarmouth now stands.

Sea levels remained high before eventually falling again later in the Bronze Age. This was also a period of favourable climate, with conditions warmer and drier than those of today. The farming communities spread steadily across the Norfolk landscape.

The region's many rivers provided the quickest and safest method of transport and it is perhaps surprising that boats and canoes of this period have not yet been discovered in Norfolk. Such evidence undoubtedly remains buried at locations beneath the peat.

In common with other parts of Britain, Norfolk saw more significant developments in the form of large visible monuments in the landscape, many of which either survive today or can be traced through archaeology. These monuments required the cooperation of large numbers of people for their construction. The evidence for social cooperation on such a scale only occurred following the stability of populations enabled by food surpluses provided by the Agricultural Revolution.

There were many burial mounds known as round barrows but, otherwise, Norfolk is not rich in the major field monuments that are more common in counties further west. Most of Norfolk's 1,200 round barrows, which can be dated from between 2880 and 2490 BC (Norwich Southern Bypass) to around 1860–1510 BC (Weasenham Lyngs), were constructed within occupied and cultivated landscapes. Many survive today as flattened earthworks, in the form of ring ditches. Such burials often occur together in cemeteries.

Other monuments known as 'henges' were round enclosures, each with a bank laying beyond an internal ditch, and were located in low-lying locations. Their function is still debated but may have related to their alignments with the heavenly cycles and in predicting the change of seasons. Seven henges are known in Norfolk, including a wooden example at Arminghall, south of Norwich.

Another form of monument was identified at Holme-next-the-Sea in 1998. Today, the location of this mysterious timber structure is on the coast, but at the time of its construction it was further inland. Its purpose remains uncertain and is a focus of continuing fascination. Despite its popular name, Seahenge was not a henge monument. Instead, the structure comprised an oval arrangement of oak posts surrounding an upside-down central oak stump. There were fifty-six posts, which had been split in half, with their flat surfaces facing inwards, creating a flat inner wall. It has been calculated that 200 people would have been involved in its construction. Modern scientific techniques have dated the monument to 2049 BC.

THE SIGNIFICANCE OF MONUMENTS IN THE LANDSCAPE

The full significance of these great monuments remains unclear. Prehistoric peoples had their own religion and mythology that has been lost to us. We don't understand how they thought although, like us today, they had their own daily problems to think about and solve. In practical terms, particularly with the advent of farming, they needed to be able to predict the passing of the seasons and observed the sun, moon, planets and stars for this purpose.

Today, we have lost the associations and meanings that people had in relation to the world around them. The arrangements of their burial mounds, henges and other field monuments provide us with some tantalising clues to their thinking. We are able to see that some natural places in the landscape had special associations to them and remained significant for long passages of time. Yet we are left to speculate the true mythology of their landscape and to fully understand what was significant to these people and why.

THE FIRST CONQUEST OF BRITAIN AND A NEW POPULATION

From around 3000 BC there was widespread disruption right across Europe. A people, known as the Yamnaya, who had originated in the Eurasian steppes between the Black Sea and Caucasus Mountains, spread outwards and started to colonise large areas of western Europe. Genetic evidence suggests that this process was not peaceful but was accompanied by a series of events, which resulted in much of the existing European farming population being wiped out. The study of ancient DNA shows that local Neolithic populations were being replaced by ones associated with the Yamnaya line.

New people arrived in Britain around 2500 BC and immediately left their mark in the archaeological record. Their presence is revealed to us by a form of pottery known as Beakers, which are a type of decorated drinking jar, sometimes with a flared rim. These 'Beaker people' were closely associated with the Yamnaya and shared many of their known traits. Their practices are evidenced in grave goods. Their Beaker pots were regularly accompanied by arrowheads, battle axes and copper daggers. Other evidence shows that they were horse-mounted warriors. Their arrival also coincided with the start of the age of metals, initially through the use of copper.

Beaker pottery is particularly well represented in Norfolk, revealing a strong presence of these new people across the area. The proximity to north-west Europe would have made this a major route for their influx into Britain. Some stayed, while others passed through to re-populate other parts of the country.

The arrival of the Beaker people had a much greater impact than any subsequent invasion in British history. Recent genetic analysis shows that the previous Neolithic population, who had introduced farming and constructed the large field monuments, all but disappeared and had been replaced by the new population within just a couple of generations.

THE FIRST USE OF BRONZE

It was from about 2500 BC that we have evidence for the first use of bronze. Metalworking was a considerable improvement over flint technology. It involved a process of smelting and casting metal in pre-shaped moulds. Objects of Early Bronze Age metalwork are well represented in Norfolk. Their findspots appear to confirm that the eastern edge of the Fens was a major regional concentration of settlement and metalworking.

Early Bronze Age burials in Norfolk were normally accompanied by modest grave goods. However, one group at Little Cressingham, situated in Breckland, to the west of Watton, near the Icknield Way and dated *c*.1600 BC, contrasts from others in this part of England. One of the barrows contains a more elaborate 'Wessex-type' burial, containing a gold plate, cylindrical gold boxes, two daggers and an exotic amber necklace. This is the most important and striking example of this form of burial from the whole of East Anglia.

The Middle Bronze Age (*c*.1500 to 1250 BC) saw innovation in the art of metalworking. New object forms appeared, including palstaves (a developed form of axe), rapiers and socketed-and-looped spearheads. In 2002 a highly unusual ceremonial example of a class of weaponry known as the dirk was discovered at Rudham, in west Norfolk.

Norfolk is exceptionally rich in metalwork of the Late Bronze Age (*c.*1250 to *c.*700 BC). The quantity, quality and variety of the metalwork is unsurpassed anywhere else in Britain and in fact provides the most profitable source of information about the Bronze Age period in Norfolk as a whole. In turn, the forms of artefact being made reflect the developments going on within society. These objects include pieces of elaborate body armour, shields and weaponry, especially spears, which collectively indicate that warfare was taking place. Swords are not common finds in Norfolk and tend to be found as fragments, most commonly in hoards. The most impressive item found in Norfolk is a beautifully crafted and decorated circular shield from Sutton, in north-east Norfolk.

There are few surviving Bronze Age settlements in Norfolk. The organic materials that people used to build their houses have left no trace for archaeologists to find. However, the discoveries of tools, weapons and pottery show that people were living right across this area.

THE IRON AGE

The start of the Iron Age in northern East Anglia dates from *c.*700 BC and lasted until the middle of the first century AD. The transition from the preceding Bronze Age was a gradual one. The period saw the steadily increased use of iron, alongside bronze, and was accompanied by more developments in society.

As the Iron Age progressed, society became organised into chiefdoms and tribes. These groupings fluctuated in size and composition over time and they were associated with territories and visible boundaries in the landscape. We can detect that there was an increase in warfare and fighting between the tribal groups.

Recent studies have revealed that the people of Norfolk and northern East Anglia, who have been called the Iceni, had a vibrant, distinct and complex culture. Religion was important to them and ritual activities were an integral part of daily life. They operated their own mature coinage system in the century preceding the Roman invasion of Britain. Many finds of horse-related objects show that the raising of horses played an important role in Iron Age Norfolk, as it continues to do in parts of East Anglia today.

By the start of the Iron Age, substantial woodland clearance was already under way. The landscape was being intensively farmed and management of the land was becoming important. In addition, the remaining ancient woodland was reduced to islands within broader areas of farmland. Heath vegetation spread as the period progressed, notably on the sandy soils of west Norfolk and in the Breckland. The southern heathlands provided grazing for sheep and horses. The extensive central claylands became more fully used during the Middle Iron Age (*c.*400–*c.*100 BC) but were not completely exploited until the Late Iron Age.

There was a major marine transgression after *c.*250 BC, which lasted through to the end of the Roman period (the early fifth century). At the time of the Roman invasion in AD 43, rivers had swelled and the wide estuary where Great Yarmouth now stands dominated the eastern approach to Norfolk. The Fenland also became much wetter.

The watery features of the Fens and River Waveney, which today define the extent of Norfolk, formed more imposing physical boundaries.

Evidence for Iron Age settlements in Norfolk is again limited. The population lived in small farmsteads spread across the landscape. At present, some 640 sites of the period have been recorded, which are recognised by their use of ditches, field systems, enclosures, trackways and stock enclosures. Signs of increasing pressure and tension between communities, resulting from a growing population, is evidenced by new land boundaries in the form of earthworks.

One of the better known of Norfolk's Iron Age farmsteads is at West Harling near Thetford, set on a gravel hillock next to the River Thet. It was surrounded in part by a bank and ditch. Here, two adjacent enclosures contained roundhouses. The site has been dated to between 510 and 380 BC, making it a Middle Iron Age settlement.

There were no towns at this time but during the Late Iron Age, larger sites developed across parts of Britain that we call *oppida*. They were centres of production and distribution and where coinage was first used. It has been suggested that some larger Norfolk sites, including the Saham Toney and Ashill area and across the Tas Valley in the east, performed a similar role to that of *oppida*. Unfortunately, none of these locations has yet been adequately investigated by archaeology.

Another category of site is that of medium-sized earthwork enclosures that are found in west Norfolk and sometimes referred to as 'hillforts'. They are Thetford Castle, Narborough, South Creake, Warham Camp and Holkham. To this list, another possible example at Bawsey may be added. This intriguing category of site once again lacks any substantial evidence from modern excavation.

They are all situated to the west of the central watershed, in west Norfolk.

Together, Norfolk's hillforts formed a chain of prominent and highly visible sites, running from the north coast, at Holkham, to the extreme south, at Thetford, which can be seen to form a north-to-south boundary, separating west from east into two distinct zones. To the east of these sites, the natural drainage flows eastwards, towards the North Sea. To the west, the natural drainage flows westwards and some of the most prominent sites and hoards of the Late Iron Age are located there.

It was during the earlier part of the first century BC that several sites, all located inside the western zone, came to prominence. The most famous of these is at Ken Hill, Snettisham, situated on the extreme western edge of Norfolk, and which had been a centre of activity since the Bronze Age. During the Late Iron Age it became a focus for the burial of precious gold and silver torcs (elaborate neck rings) and other material unequalled anywhere else in the country. Material from the site provides evidence for contact with the Mediterranean world at this early time, with coins from Carthage, Gaul (France), Greece and other parts of Britain. The presence of this material suggests that there would have been a trading port in the near vicinity, perhaps located on the Wash adjacent to Snettisham or perhaps further north in the Brancaster area. The carefully structured method of the hoard deposits indicates that this was a ritual site and that Snettisham was a focus of religious activity of international attention, exercising influence over a very wide area.

It is important to consider the distribution of torcs in their own right. More torcs have been found in East Anglia than in the rest of Britain, with most of them coming from Norfolk. The greatest concentration was at Ken

Hill, Snettisham, while many others have also come from the extreme west of Norfolk, including North Creake, Sedgeford, Bawsey, Hockham, Hevingham and Marham. The overall practice of torc burial in Britain can be closely associated with west Norfolk. It may also be noted that a number of hoards of Late Iron Age horse equipment have been found in the county's western zone. These come from Ovington, Ringstead, Quidney Farm Saham Toney, Whinburgh and Carleton Rode.

Another prominent Late Iron Age site in west Norfolk was at Sedgeford, where unusually rich objects, including coin deposits, have been discovered over a number of years. Further south, Bawsey, near King's Lynn, has yielded electrum and gold torcs, torc fragments and decorative pieces of horse harness. Fincham is another site where exceptional material has been found.

This period also marks the first time that Thetford came to prominence. The remarkable enclosure discovered at Gallows Hill, Thetford, developed into a grand ceremonial tribal centre during the early first century. Set on high ground, it was situated at a strategic location of regional importance. It dominated both land and river routes at a crossing point between the ancient trackway known as the Icknield Way and the Thet and Little Ouse rivers. This would have been the major entry point into Iceni territory. The Gallows Hill site watched over, and was visible to, people entering and leaving the area and controlled the movement of people in and out of the land of the Iceni.

IRON AGE SOCIETY

It was the Romans, at the time of the Roman conquest, who adopted tribal names for their administrative subdivisions of Britain, based on what they considered to be existing tribal areas. We are told by the Roman historian Tacitus that the area of Norfolk was inhabited by the Iceni tribe, whose territory also covered parts of Suffolk and Cambridgeshire. In reality, the social and political structure of Late Iron Age Britain was far more complex than this basic 'tribal map' implies. We should envisage a more decentralised pattern of social organisation. What we simplistically refer to as the Iceni would have comprised a series of small-scale groupings based on family ties and client networks, each with its own leader, but then coming together with their neighbours under a single leader at times of extreme stress.

Archaeology is today showing how the people of this area were different in many ways to those in other parts of Britain, as witnessed through their distinct material culture. While much of the country was ruled by kings or chieftains, the evidence from northern East Anglia is now pointing to a more egalitarian society.

Archaeology is also showing us that this was a sophisticated society. Unfortunately, people did not use writing and so much of their way of life is lost to us. But the study of their settlements and everyday objects indicates that they had a complex set of beliefs and rituals and a remarkable richness and symbolism in their art. They were already using their own complex coinage system before the arrival of the Romans and there are clues in the coinage suggesting that they had a close association with continental Germanic peoples at this time.

At the time of the Roman conquest in AD 43, it is clear that the people of Iron Age Norfolk had an identity distinct from other tribal peoples. At this stage the population was intentionally looking inward from the rest of Britain and perhaps outwards towards Europe. Not only did they manifest their identity through their material culture and behaviour, it appears that they were also intentionally rejecting materials associated with both other regional peoples and with the Roman way of life, including the use of Roman pottery and other imported luxury items, which were being adopted in other parts of southern England.

These fiercely independent people were initially to remain separate from events in the rest of Britain for some seventeen years after the Roman invasion; on the periphery, or border, of the new Roman province. Tragic events then intervened, which drew Norfolk to centre stage and to national attention.

3

THE ROMANS

43–410

With the Roman conquest of Britain in AD 43, Britain formally became part of the Roman Empire. In some aspects of daily existence, life continued much as it had before. But the Romans imposed changes and introduced some very different ideas. They created towns, together with stone and brick buildings, an Empire-wide coinage system and their own religious beliefs. They brought industrial-scale production of disposable items and trade on a scale not seen before. They also introduced their imperial political system. Their use of writing stimulated a new source of evidence valued by today's historians and through this medium they have introduced us to the first named people who lived in the area.

The southern and eastern coastal counties of Britain had never been isolated from continental Europe and its influences. There had been contact with the Mediterranean world prior to the Roman invasion, as shown by objects and coins imported to Norfolk during the Iron Age. The world of Rome had established and maintained political influence and commercial ties with southern England.

The area occupied by the people referred to as the Iceni, with Norfolk at its heart, was not an initial priority for the Romans. It remained largely independent, with the status of a client state on the periphery, while the main conquest of Britain was being pursued. As a consequence, Norfolk's Iron Age lasted some seventeen years longer than elsewhere in Britain. It finally came to a sudden and brutal end with the Boudican uprising in AD 60.

Once Norfolk was made part of the Roman province, it was to remain under imperial rule for a further 350 years. This should not, therefore, be considered as a single episode and was subject to changes and developments over that time. There was initially a degree of continuity of lifestyle and settlement from the preceding Iron Age. Across most of the area, and for much of the population, there was little change until the third and fourth centuries. While the local population remained stable, peoples also came in from other parts of the Empire through trade links and as auxiliaries in the army to protect our shores. In this way, some parts of the area became cosmopolitan.

Roman Norfolk has left a strong visible legacy on today's landscape. Perhaps the most spectacular examples are in the east of the county, where substantial walls survive above the ground at both the Saxon Shore site of Burgh Castle, to the south of Great Yarmouth, and at the town of *Venta Icenorum* at Caistor St Edmund, south of Norwich. Other sites are still recognisable above ground to a varying extent. Some are visible and survive in other ways, through the reuse of their building materials. Churches in the vicinity of the late Roman sites at Brancaster in north Norfolk and Reedham in the east contain prolific quantities of building stone and tile from Roman buildings that have otherwise disappeared.

In the previous chapter it was observed that Late Iron Age society comprised a number of sub-regional groupings and that significant differences in terms of sites, monuments and wealth existed between the west and the east of the county. The same dichotomy was to continue through Roman Norfolk and was manifested in a number of ways.

THE BOUDICA STORY

At the outset of the Roman conquest, the area of Norfolk was on the periphery of the part of Britain considered to be of most strategic importance to the Romans. The Iceni of northern East Anglia entered into a treaty relationship with Rome, with the status of a 'client kingdom'. Such an arrangement was not unique to the Iceni and 'client kingdoms' were often strategically positioned around the edges of Rome's troublesome frontiers. In this way they retained Roman protection while maintaining a degree of independence.

The first reference we have to a leader of the Iceni is a coin carrying the name of Prasutagus. It is possible that this individual may have been raised to the status of tribal leader by the Romans, who needed an appropriate local person with whom they could conduct political relations. The coin was struck in silver and in the style of Roman coins of emperors Claudius and Nero who ruled at that time. Its Latin inscription reads, SVB RI PRASTO ESICO FECIT, which means 'under King Prasutagus, Esico (the moneyer) made me'.

The wife of Prasutagus was Boudica, who has become one of the most famous characters from world history. On her husband's death, Boudica became queen of the Iceni. We know tantalisingly little about her background. She would have been an important individual and can be considered an aristocrat within local society. Both she and Prasutagus must have shown themselves to be receptive to Roman culture and probably dressed and behaved in a way that reflected Roman fashions. The Roman historian Dio Cassius, writing in the late second, early third century, provided the following description of her:

She was very tall and severe.
Her gaze was penetrating and her voice was harsh.
She grew long red hair that fell to her hips
And wore a large golden torc
And a vast patterned cloak with a thick plaid fastened
over it.

When Prasutagus died in AD 60, he attempted to bequeath half of his estate to his family rather than to the Roman Emperor. Catus Decianus, Procurator of Britain, was sent to the region to assert the authority of the Emperor. He committed outrages against the queen and her two daughters, setting in motion a train of events that led to the tribal uprising of AD 60–61.

Boudica led the Iceni from their Norfolk homeland, together with their allies, south to the Roman capital at *Camulodunum*. The town was razed to the ground and a statue of the Emperor Claudius demolished. Boudica's army then proceeded to destroy the Roman towns at London and Verulamium (St Albans) before eventually being lured to battle and to defeat at a now-lost site, possibly near Mancetter in the Midlands.

By the time of Boudica the previously important sites of west Norfolk, such as Snettisham, had declined and there is more evidence of settlements developing further east. Sites in the Breckland at Saham Toney, Ashill and Thetford, in south Norfolk at Wicklewood and in east Norfolk, became more prominent. Archaeological discoveries, in the form of buried coin and metalwork hoards, suggest that the focus of Boudica's uprising occurred in central-south Norfolk. One of these deposits from Crownthorpe, near Wymondham, provides direct evidence of one of Boudica's supporters.

The Crownthorpe Hoard comprised seven bronze vessels and had been deliberately hidden. It contained a bowl and saucepan, both imported from Italy, together with other vessels and two delightful drinking cups, together representing a drinking set of the type commonly used within a Roman household. These vessels show that the owner had adopted Roman ways. If the owner had buried his treasure while fleeing Boudica's anti-Roman rebels, intent on revenge against those showing pro-Roman sympathies, he was presumably caught and did not survive to recover his possessions.

The Boudican episode provides a fascinating insight into the emerging Roman province of Britain. Writing about the events, the Roman historians Tacitus and Cassius Dio provide historical information for a period that otherwise relies heavily on archaeology. If we look at the episode in its wider context, it is interesting to note that the manifestation of a patriotic tribal chieftain, at a key moment in history, is not unique to Britain. Such charismatic leaders are known in every other part of the Roman Empire, emerging when their homeland was initially threatened by Roman aggression. Others include Jugurtha in Numidia (Libya), Ambiorix in Belgium, Dumnorix and Vercingetorix in France, Viriathus in Portugal and Arminius in Germany, to name but a few. In England, Boudica's name has lived on as a patriotic rallying point throughout the centuries. Today, her name has even become a highly popular marketing brand, especially across the east of England.

THE YEARS AFTER BOUDICA

The Romans spent the immediate post-conquest years strengthening their control of Britain. In Norfolk, they erected garrison forts at strategic intervals across the countryside. Woodcock Hall, at Saham Toney in Breckland, was an early fort of the Claudian period (41–54) constructed on a bluff, south of the River Blackwater. A second fort close by at Threxton was probably constructed in the aftermath of the Boudican uprising. Another potential early fort has been identified nearby at Ashill, north-west of Saham Toney.

Aerial photography has revealed the location of an early fort at Swanton Morley, again in Breckland, next to the Romano-British small town of Billingford. The characteristic 'playing card' shape was clearly outlined, as was a defensive triple-ditch system, which has also been associated with several forts of this date across East Anglia.

A large cropmark enclosure has been identified west of Horstead, north of Norwich. Its size suggests that a detachment of legionary size could have used it, possibly as a temporary marching camp. It is likely that a very substantial force of this type would have been involved in pacifying the area following the Boudican troubles. Another marching camp has been discovered at Barton Bendish. Ditches indicate another possible installation to the north of Norwich at Scottow, while pieces of Roman military equipment have been found at the sites of Great Walsingham, Gallows Hill in Thetford, Scole and Caistor St Edmund.

Some other finds, especially early Roman coin types normally associated with the army, have more coastally associated findspots. These may indicate military movements in the area in the aftermath of the rebellion.

Landings between Burgh Castle in the east and Heacham in the west may have served to supply and reinforce troops advancing north overland.

THE LAND

At this time, parts of the northern coastline between Holme-next-the-Sea and Happisburgh lay to the north of its present position. The period saw both marine transgressions and recessions, the latter enabling people to move west into the Fenland. The east, where Great Yarmouth now stands, was still open water and the landscape was dominated by the Great Estuary that extended some 20km inland, fed by rivers that included the Yare, Bure and Waveney. To the north, the region of Flegg was a large island and, to the south, Lothingland formed a long peninsula. The estuary and its rivers were an attractive focus to the Romans for local and long-distance trade.

The Romans themselves also made an impression on the physical landscape during the later first and second centuries. They appear to have imposed an alignment of features including lengths of Roman road, lanes, agricultural trackways and some field boundaries, which were set out in a grand formal design. Together, they appear to form a large-scale formal layout established in the aftermath of the Roman conquest.

An immediate consequence of the Boudican rebellion was a depopulation of the region. We are told by Tacitus that the scale of local casualties was very high and a great many agricultural workers were lost, either killed during the battles or subsequently taken away as slaves. It would have taken decades for the population to return to its former levels. Life in the countryside was drastically affected and its inhabitants struggled to recover, possibly through into the second century.

The situation in the far west of Norfolk was quite different. A large imperial estate was established early on across part of the Fenland, extending from Denver in the south west, and westwards through Lincolnshire. It was administered from the period of Hadrian (117–38) from a site in the central Fenland, probably at Stonea (Cambridgeshire). Many of the sites of the Norfolk fen-edge would have come under its control, sharing an economy based on intensive stock rearing and wool production.

SETTLEMENT

One of the most significant changes under the Romans was the introduction of towns. The new administration needed a regional centre for government, which was established at Caistor St Edmund, just south of where Norwich later grew up. The chosen location had been a focus of settlement from Neolithic times through to the Iron Age. It had natural advantages, situated just off of the adjacent clay soils and next to the River Tas. This location facilitated both land transport and river links to eastern coastal ports.

The initial street layout has been dated to the Flavian period (69–96). Known as *Venta Icenorum*, this was the largest town in northern East Anglia and served as the regional *civitas capital*. During the last quarter of the fourth century it was reduced in size by about a half, to 14 hectares (35 acres) by the construction of a massive defensive flint wall.

Venta was, however, a modest town by Roman standards. It was smaller than other Romano-British regional capitals; only about half the size of Roman Colchester.

It lacks evidence for major investment in its Roman-style public buildings. Neither was it rich in material terms. Roman imported items, such as wine amphorae and Samian Ware pottery, which are common elsewhere in Britain, are rare finds at the site. Industrial activity too was modest and the town layout included many open spaces without buildings.

The evidence from *Venta Icenorum* is consistent with the situation in Late Iron Age Norfolk, whereby the local population were reluctant to adopt Roman ways of doing things. It suggests that the Iceni were still choosing to reject the imposed Roman lifestyle, or at least accepting it half-heartedly. They preferred to express their own identity wherever possible and to maintain their own distinct way of life. Resistance to the standard model of romanisation would have been even more important to them in the aftermath of their bitter defeat in AD 61.

Elsewhere, the post-conquest years saw the growth of a network of Romano-British small towns across Norfolk. These medium-sized settlements are found at regular intervals of between 15 and 20km and were generally situated at route centres. They provided a whole range of functions that facilitated the working of Roman Norfolk. A number, including Crownthorpe, Needham, Ditchingham and Great Walsingham, show evidence of earlier occupation, during the Late Iron Age, in the form of coins and other objects. These settlements are mainly located in the east and south-east.

The lack of native building stone can be apparent in the remains of these settlements. At Great Walsingham, extensive spreads of tiles used on roofs and heating ducts betray the existence of buildings, the walls of which had been made from timber and other organic materials that have not survived.

To the north of *Venta Icenorum* was the small town of Brampton, which grew up at a crossroads and river crossing. An industrial suburb developed and Brampton became a major producer of pottery, with over 140 kilns. These supplied a local market as well as a more distant one. Brampton products have been found as far afield as the Antonine Wall, near Edinburgh.

Venta Icenorum appears to have provided a market focus in the east of Norfolk but there is a noticeable difference in the west, where there is an absence of small towns. In the south-west, there is a single small town at Denver, in the vicinity of where the Imperial Estate would have been located. Denver lacked development seen elsewhere, which may have been because the normal town functions were provided by the estate and its administration. The economic structure in the west clearly differed from that evidenced in the rest of Norfolk and appears to have been specifically based on large-scale farming operations, centred in the nearby Fenland and on the villas in the later period.

In many parts there was initially very little change in the lifestyle from that of the Iron Age; the landscape covered by a network of small farms. The economy was based on small basic rural settlements such as that excavated at Spong Hill in North Elmham and continued as before.

In the west, a system of individual settlement plots and allotments has been identified at Park Farm, Snettisham, through a dense system of cropmarks, which can be traced for over 3km. These settlements had grown up before the end of the first century AD on either side of the River Ingol. There was a noticeable decline in activity there during the third century.

Further south, the southern fen-edge experienced an expansion of settlement as the Roman period progressed. An extensive rural settlement has been investigated at

Watlington, associated with stock rearing and agriculture. This appears to have been a 'low order' settlement, representing activity over a period of some 400 years. It expanded during the later second and third centuries, when a regular field system was also established.

COMMUNICATIONS

One of the most widespread and visible legacies of the Roman occupation is the network of roads. In the years after the invasion the Romans strengthened their control and constructed roads in order to speed up movements of troops, supplies and communications, to and from other parts of the province. The network was largely established in the half century between the conquest and the end of the first century.

Evidence for Roman roads in Norfolk is contained in the Roman document known as the Antonine Itinerary, which outlines journeys planned by the Emperor Caracalla (AD 211–217). Route IX describes a road from *Venta Icenorum* to London. Route V runs from London to Cambridge, and mentions the Norfolk sites of *Villa Faustini* (thought to be Scole) and *Venta Icenorum*.

Venta Icenorum formed the hub of the road system in the east, as well as being at the centre of a network of river routes stretching east to the Great Estuary and the sea beyond. The movement of goods by road was slow and expensive, while water transport through the extensive network of rivers and long coastline was quicker, much more efficient and also safer. The Great Estuary allowed maritime transport to penetrate far inland by medium-sized boats and barges. *Venta Icenorum* acted as a redistribution centre, where goods were transferred from barges to land transport.

The Fen Causeway ran directly west from *Venta*, passing through Crownthorpe, Threxton and Denver, and is still visible across the landscape as a band of orange gravel in places. In central-west Norfolk, the Peddars Way ran north from Bildeston in Suffolk, cutting through Breckland and passing through Threxton towards Holme-next-the-Sea, in the extreme north-west. It is thought that this must have been a ferry point for vessels, perhaps of military origin, to cross the Wash into Lincolnshire.

RELIGION

Religion played an important role, permeating all aspects of everyday life, just as it had in the Iron Age. The Romans were polytheist, with a range of their own gods and goddesses. They did not attempt to convert the conquered population to their religion. Instead, they pursued a policy of religious tolerance that helped the integration between themselves and the people of the area. In time, local Celtic gods became associated with their Roman counterparts, becoming combined into a 'Romano-Celtic' religion.

A range of objects of the period associated with religious practices have been found right across Norfolk with widespread evidence for worship of the major Roman state gods, Jupiter, Juno and Minerva. Other Roman gods such as Mars and Mercury are similarly well represented.

A number of Iron Age sites associated with religious or ritual behaviour continued to have a similar function into the Roman period, such as Ken Hill, Snettisham. Romano-British temples have been found at Caistor St Edmund, Crownthorpe, Great Walsingham and Hockwold-cum-Wilton, all of which were towns. Temple sites would have attracted people from wide areas and also served as the focus of periodic fairs and festivals, as well as the locations for markets and commercial activity. These religious practices once again manifest sub-regional differences.

The material evidence is able to show that different cults existed across parts of Norfolk. For example, cult objects linked with the deities Pan, Faunus and Bacchus cover much of Norfolk, but with the notable exception of the far west and Fenland. In contrast, cult figurines depicting a raven are clustered in north-east Norfolk. It has also been shown that a particular zoomorphic form of brooch, known as the 'horse and rider', is often found in association with Norfolk's temples.

Two objects found in the county give us an insight into how people thought about the gods at this time. Both are metal items and were engraved by individuals as direct communications with the gods. The first is a lead curse tablet, known as a *defixio*, which was found on the bank of the River Tas, at Caistor St Edmund. This had been tightly rolled up and dedicated to the God Neptune. Unrolled, it shows an inscription on one side. It requests the help of Neptune to seek out a thief and recover a list of stolen items that include a wreath, bracelets, a cap, a mirror, a headdress, a pair of leggings and ten pewter vessels. Unfortunately, the name of the writer has not been recorded.

The second object is known as a *lamella*; a very rare form of amulet made from a thin sheet of metal, which was worn as a charm against evil. Magical protective spells were written on one side and it was then rolled up to contain the magic and worn around the neck. This example was found at Billingford in central Norfolk and is only the fourth such gold example ever to be recorded from Roman Britain. It is made from a gold sheet and has been lightly inscribed with writing in a mixture of Greek and Latin characters and magic symbols. The writer signed himself

'*Tiberius Claudius Similis, son of Herennia Marcellina*'. Similis has used the charm to call on the protection of Abrasax, who was an eastern deity, often depicted as having the head of a cockerel and with snakes for legs. Such charms indicate the presence of small immigrant communities in Roman Britain. It is thought that Similis was not British by birth and that he may have originated from Lower Germany.

Somewhat surprisingly, there is a lack of evidence for Christianity having been practiced in Roman Norfolk. This situation can be contrasted with that in adjacent Suffolk and Cambridgeshire, where numerous finds of early Christian association have been made.

TRADE AND THE ECONOMY

The Romans brought with them a mature coinage system that operated across the whole Mediterranean world. Coin use remained slight in the British countryside for many years after the invasion, probably until the second half of the third century. The new coinage served to stimulate and facilitate commerce in some specific locations such as towns, markets and fairs.

The economy of Roman Norfolk was largely agricultural and was geared towards food production. The extensive coastline also supported a fishing industry. Evidence for a range of other industries has come from archaeological excavations. Digs at the small towns of Scole and Brampton have revealed evidence of industrial activities, including iron and bronze working, leatherworking, tanning and malting. Pottery was manufactured right across the area, with wares for both local use and for export to other parts of Britain.

Evidence of other more specialist craft activities have also been discovered. Glass was produced at *Venta Icenorum* and iron smelting was undertaken at Ashwicken, Hevingham, Aylsham and other sites along the Holt–Cromer ridge. The materials of a jeweller's workshop were found at Snettisham.

In the west, there is evidence for manufacturing on a large scale being focused in the area of the Nar Valley, including pottery production and iron smelting. Here, activity developed across the eastern offshoot of the Fenland basin, some 5km south of King's Lynn. This industrial focus, which provided products and services for a wide area, is quite different from anything known in the east of Norfolk. As yet, investigation into this fascinating area is only at an early stage.

THE LATER ROMAN SITUATION

The later centuries of Roman rule are associated with new developments. Sea levels fell and a sandbank started to emerge at the mouth of the Great Estuary, where Great Yarmouth now stands, although there was no stable land for settlement there at that time. The main period of villa construction was during the third and fourth centuries. Many of Norfolk's earlier smallholdings can be seen to have developed into larger and more profitable farms. However, Norfolk was not rich in these country houses, especially those manifesting signs of great wealth or ostentation in design. It was in the west that the main focus of villa construction occurred, with a bigger concentration of substantial Roman rural buildings in north-west Norfolk than in any other part of the county. Villa owners favoured slopes overlooking valleys at Hunstanton, Heacham and

Snettisham. There is a chain of ten villas situated between Gayton Thorpe and Heacham, close to the Icknield Way. At Park Farm, Snettisham, a villa estate grew up and replaced the previous farming system of smaller settlement plots.

Although they have been subject to very little excavation, the floruit of these grand country houses appears to have been in the third and early fourth centuries. They all show a modest amount of luxury, less so than across much of southern Britain, and appear to have been located at the centres of individual agricultural estates. Each of these would probably have farmed several thousand acres.

It was during the final century and a half of Roman rule that large walled sites were constructed around the east coast and further inland. The coastal sites are associated with the defensive system known as the Saxon Shore. This chain of forts and signal stations, built during the later third and fourth centuries AD, stretched from Portchester in Hampshire eastwards and northwards, to embrace Norfolk, whose sites include Burgh Castle, Caister-on-Sea and Brancaster. Another might have existed at Reedham, as evidenced by the prolific Roman building materials left behind, although no intact remains survive above ground today. Inland, the walls of *Venta Icenorum* were also built at this time, towards the end of the third century.

The construction of all these massive flint and stone sites involved organisation of labour on a large scale. This in turn indicates the presence, or injection, of significant wealth and financial investment into the region during the third and fourth centuries. All of these sites, except for Brancaster, are concentrated in the east of the county.

The importance of continental trade into the Great Estuary continued right through to the final decades of Roman Norfolk. Fragments of imported exotic glass vessels, including examples from nearby Gallia Belgica

(Belgium) and more distant Egypt, have been found. Although there is no surviving evidence for a Roman port in western Norfolk, there would have been a need for such a facility in the vicinity of the Wash through which agricultural production from that area would have needed to be exported.

THE END OF ROMAN NORFOLK

A late third-century document written to the Emperor Constantius (AD 305–06) talks of Britain's benefits to the Empire as having been the production of cereals of all kinds and that it was well provided with harbours. This brief description provides a simple summary of Roman Norfolk's importance within Roman Britain, which was perhaps greater than has previously been appreciated. Evidence from across the county shows how Roman Norfolk was geared toward agricultural production, while the important trade routes out of east Norfolk, via the Great Estuary, and from western Norfolk, via the Wash, were in direct proximity to the major trade routes associated with the Rhine mouth and its vicinity.

There is in fact evidence for a great concentration of wealth in northern East Anglia in the final decades of Roman Britain. Remarkable discoveries of treasure have been made across the region over the last eighty years. In 1942 a hoard of late Roman silver objects was found on the fen-edge at Mildenhall, Suffolk. Three decades later a hoard of early Christian gold and silver objects was found at Water Newton, Cambridgeshire. In 1979 a deposit of gold finger rings, silver objects, beads and gems was discovered at Thetford. In 1992 an even more spectacular find was made at Hoxne in north Suffolk. The Hoxne

Treasure was the largest hoard of gold and silver ever found on British soil.

These rich deposits all tend to be found on and around the borders of Norfolk. They represent accumulations of precious metals and fine objects, including items of exceptionally high-quality workmanship. The final decades of the fourth and early fifth centuries were troubled times, for there was a climate of political uncertainty as the Roman army was being withdrawn from Britain to defend the central Empire on mainland Europe. Some rich people were burying their wealth in the ground for safekeeping, as Roman administration was breaking down.

In most respects, it must be concluded that the area of Norfolk was not at all remarkable during the Roman period. Its largest town, at Caistor St Edmund, was much smaller than other towns of the south and east of England, such as Lincoln, Leicester and Colchester. *Venta Icenorum* can be characterised as a microcosm of Roman Norfolk, lacking rich Mediterranean imports, with an absence of fine mosaics and other daily comforts. In the later period, Norfolk lacked the numbers of rich villas found elsewhere across lowland Britain. Roman Norfolk's material culture, which is noteworthy in its quantity, comprises largely ordinary domestic everyday items and in general terms lacks richness or high quality.

The late Roman treasure deposits, found around the county's borders, present a puzzling anomaly. Roman Norfolk was not otherwise showing visible signs of wealth, although the ability to undertake a building programme involving the construction of walls around key sites shows that wealth was present in the vicinity. Undoubtedly, the region's agriculture and population had recovered following their mid-first century decline and participated in the substantial export of produce, especially via the Great Estuary. Agriculture and the Roman countryside always played a fundamental role in relation to both Roman politics and the Roman economy and the possession of land equated to social standing and wealth. Norfolk's rural assets, its position as a borderland and its great eastern waterway, were significant local factors. It must be inferred that some very wealthy families of landowners lived in the region, although evidence for their presence remains to be found.

The end of Roman presence in Britain has been dated to 410, when the Emperor Honorius (393–423) withdrew the last remnants of the army. Saxon raids were already gathering pace. They were arriving in the east of England in increasing numbers, not just as raiders but as invaders and settlers.

4

THE ANGLO-SAXONS
AND VIKINGS

410–1066

The withdrawal of the Romans from Britain in 410 was
followed by a period for which we have fewer historical
accounts to draw on. Reading and writing declined and,
once again, we rely heavily on the contribution of archaeology for an interpretation of events and how people lived.
Fortunately, Norfolk is rich in evidence for these otherwise
'Dark Ages'. The culture associated with the Roman world
eventually fell away and was subsumed by new practices.
The old political structure declined and town life, together
with the daily comforts associated with the Classical world,
such as plumbing and bathing, disappeared. Roman trading networks broke down and the supply of luxury goods
to Britain ceased.

Norfolk's attention now switches eastwards, across
the North Sea. Its history again became heavily associated with events on the European mainland. The region
was to absorb new cultural influences, along with physical
migration of foreign peoples, which in turn introduced significant developments. During the half century following

the disappearance of Roman authority there were migrations of Angles and Saxons from Germany and Scandinavia
and Jutes from Denmark and Germany, who began to
occupy Britain, with the east receiving the main impact of
the invasions. As Norfolk and East Anglia absorbed these
migrations its population became more diverse, as did its
language and religious beliefs.

It is likely that there would have been a gradual period
of transition from the Roman way of life, perhaps lasting for several generations. During this time there would
have been a steady integration of the new settlers with the
native population. The traditional narrative of these times
tells of a series of kings and warlords rising to prominence
as the fifth century progressed. By around AD 500 the
Anglo-Saxon areas of Norfolk and Suffolk were attain-
ing their own identity. The native British people appear
to have been absorbed into the culture and pagan religion of the new settlers. Their old established Latin and
Celtic languages disappeared and were replaced by a new
Germanic-derived Anglo-Saxon language.

The most important aspect of Norfolk's Anglo-Saxon
archaeology is the large number of their cemeteries found
here. Although they have been discovered right across East
Anglia, Norfolk is especially rich in these sites. In recent
years, this evidence has been supplemented by a series of
exceptional finds, made by metal detectorists. The study
of the cemeteries is now key to any understanding of the
Anglo-Saxons in England. This form of evidence alone
does not fully reflect the nature of everyday domestic life,
although, in the absence of other forms of evidence, it does
provide an idea of where their settlements were located.
Relatively little structural evidence for buildings at this
time survives above ground level, partly because people
did not build houses in stone and because subsequent

intense arable land use has removed traces of their flimsy wooden structures.

THE KINGDOM OF EAST ANGLIA

During the fifth century the area of Norfolk was populated by many small tribal groupings, for which we have little detail. These groups eventually came together as the Anglo-Saxon Kingdom of East Anglia, which was formed in the first half of the sixth century, at the start of what has been called the Heroic Age. Norfolk at this time became part of a much larger entity, as the kingdom embraced both Norfolk and Suffolk, whose histories became entwined, and established the emergence of the East Angles.

The kingdom was initially ruled by the Wuffingas, who are thought to have been descended from Scandinavian invaders, who settled in the region around the year 500. King Wehha was the first ruler of East Anglia, probably from around 550. It was his son Wuffa who gave his name to the royal line. Wuffa was succeeded by his son Tyttla, who was subsequently followed by his son Raedwald, in 599. It is Raedwald who we associate with the famous and spectacular ship burial at Sutton Hoo in Suffolk. We know that he died in 624, which closely aligns with the archaeological evidence at the site. The Wuffingas continued to rule through the seventh and eighth centuries.

Beonna became King of East Anglia in 749 and ruled until *c.*760. Little is known of his reign although in recent years we have been able to learn more about him through a study of his coins. Beonna was the first ruler of East Anglia whose coinage included both his name and title.

When King Aethelberht was killed by the Mercians in 794, East Anglia fell to the power of Mercia. The kingdom was able to briefly reassert its independence again for a while under Eadwald in 796.

Very occasionally, archaeology is able to provide deeper insight into the lives of individuals from these distant times. In 1999 a discovery in a field situated a few miles to the east of Norwich provided just such an opportunity. The find in question was an unusual but clearly high status and valuable gold seal matrix of the Middle Anglo-Saxon period. Astonishingly, this has been found to have belonged to an important historical figure, Queen Balthild (626/7–680), who was the wife and queen of Clovis II, King of Burgundy and Neustria (r. 639–658). Balthild is known to have been an Anglo-Saxon of elite birth, perhaps a relative of King Ricberht of East Anglia (r. 627–30) and a native of this part of Britain before her marriage. After the death of her husband she retired to a convent, where she dedicated her remaining years to the service of the poor. Balthild was made a saint following her death in eastern France in 680. Exactly why her personal seal matrix was found in Norfolk and not France remains a puzzle. It is possible that this intimate item may have been returned to her birth family, who were still living in East Anglia, after her death.

SETTLEMENT

The departure of the Romans had eventually led to a cessation of urban life in Britain. Their towns and fortifications fell into decay and the settlement pattern associated with Roman administration broke down. The major Roman town in the region at Caistor St Edmund went out of use and people moved away to locations in the vicinity, beyond its walls.

Settlements in the fifth and sixth centuries were dispersed in the landscape. They favoured the lighter, well-drained soils within river valleys. Their cemeteries were located close to the settlements. New forms of cremation cemetery were used by the Anglo-Saxons. This development is significant because it provides evidence about the Anglo-Saxon population and their pagan practices. These cemeteries, which contain decorative cremation urns, are found right across what had been the old Icenian territory, covering Norfolk and beyond.

In the absence of other forms of evidence, these burial grounds provide an indication where early villages and the main foci of occupation were situated. Major cemeteries are known at Markshall and Illington, with others known at Morningthorpe, Brooke, Kenninghall and Sporle. At Spong Hill, in central Norfolk, the largest of the region's known Anglo-Saxon cemeteries, fieldwork between 1972 and 1981 revealed 2,259 cremations and fifty-seven inhumation burials. The cemetery was in use for 150 years and is thought to have served a number of communities in the vicinity.

Another cemetery has been excavated at Caistor St Edmund, immediately adjacent to the walls of the old Roman town. Archaeological finds, including coins, indicate the presence of communities living around, but outside, the former town, with continued presence across the surrounding area through the seventh, eighth and ninth centuries. It appears that the walled area provided a focus in the landscape but it is uncertain what role it played at that time. Somewhat later, it may have been part of a monastic foundation associated with an early church on the site, perhaps beneath the eleventh-century church of St Edmund, which is located within the town walls.

These cemeteries were no longer used from the period when Christianity became established during the seventh century. At this same time, it is apparent that settlements were becoming more nucleated in form and were established across more varied locations.

The Anglo-Saxons lived basic lives as simple farmers. Their houses were built in timber and thatch and formed small settlements. There were no towns through the fifth and sixth centuries but we can date the establishment of villages in Norfolk to the years between *c.*600 and *c.*800. It is perhaps surprising to realise that so many of today's villages were founded during those years. It was only in the later Anglo-Saxon period that the first towns emerged, together with a related growth of markets for trade, which were also associated with the increasing agricultural prosperity across the area.

Norfolk's population grew steadily from the seventh century onwards. As it developed, Anglo-Saxon settlement was not static. Once founded, villages expanded, sometimes contracted, and frequently shifted site. The most common form of domestic dwelling of the period was the *grubenhaus*, or sunken hut, in which rectangular hollows were dug, above which a suspended floor was sometimes inserted.

THE FIRST TOWNS

The main towns of Anglo-Saxon Norfolk were Thetford and Norwich. In the eighth century both consisted of just a few small dispersed settlements. They both saw Viking activity from the ninth century. Together with Yarmouth, they had established thriving merchant communities by the time of the Norman Conquest in the mid-eleventh century. None of them were planned towns but developed as thriving commercial and fishing centres respectively.

Norwich was already Norfolk's most important town. Its earliest evidence comes from around the eighth–ninth centuries. New Danish settlement in the area during the ninth century was a boost for the town's early development and it quickly became a significant regional focus. These early Scandinavian influences survive in the form of today's street names, notably those ending in –*gate* (street), such as Finkelgate and Fishergate. The earliest reference to the town's name is found on a coin of Aethelstan (r. 924–39), inscribed as *Norvic*.

Thetford was one of the largest and most important towns in the whole country from the ninth to the eleventh century. It was a bustling, busy centre of production and crafts. Excavation has shown how its roads were gravelled and its wooden houses were separated by individual fenced plots. In 1066 it had a population of over 4,000, placing it in the same league as York and Lincoln, as well as Norwich.

Norfolk's foremost early towns were to have contrasting futures. Norwich went on to have an enduring importance while Thetford was to suffer a decline after just a couple of centuries, despite its strategic location as an entry point to the county.

At the east coast, a sandbank had emerged within the mouth of the Great Estuary, providing new land that was soon occupied. The first settlement at what was to become Yarmouth was a seasonal one. Fishermen stayed there as they followed the herring down the east coast of Britain and needed protection from the sea. Their huts and homes grew into the first town on the spot. The settlers originally built on the highest part of the sandbank; an area now called Fullers Hill. It subsequently remained at the heart of the medieval town.

Yarmouth developed rapidly on the part of the growing sandbank that offered most protection from the sea, as the importance of the fishing industry expanded. The small fishing village quickly became a town and spread southwards following the course of the River Yare. Goods were loaded and unloaded from quays built into the riverside.

There was a steady growth of settlement throughout Norfolk during the eighth century, which was coupled with an increased Scandinavian and more general European presence, especially at Norwich. The economic prosperity of the region and the construction of timber buildings reflected more associations with the Low Countries and Scandinavia than with other parts of England at the time.

The spread of Anglo-Saxon settlement is indicated by the distribution of archaeological objects, especially pottery, right across the county. Evidence for specific sites is also indicated in over seventy place names ending in – *ham*. Those with such names often developed into later medieval market towns. By 1066 small markets, many of which were precursors to today's towns, were appearing, including Holt, Dunham and Litcham, all of which are mentioned in Domesday Book.

RELIGION

We have only slight evidence for what happened to the Christian religion after the Romans withdrew from Britain at the start of the fifth century. We do know that it was nearly 200 years later that it was reintroduced to England with the mission of Augustine in 597. It spread from Kent to other parts of the country during the sixth and early seventh centuries. Eorpwald became King of East Anglia on the death of Raedwald in 624 and he was converted to

Christianity in 627. It was under Sigeberht (d. 641) that the region was brought permanently to Christianity and under whom the Burgundian missionary Felix became the first bishop of the East Angles.

The Irish monks Fursa and Foillan came to East Anglia from Ireland in the 630s. They established a monastery at a place called Cnobheresburgh, which is thought to be the site of Burgh Castle in Norfolk, adjacent to the earlier Late Roman fortification. What is thought to be a Christian cemetery of seventh- to tenth-century date was discovered there during excavations in the 1950s and '60s. Post-Roman clay floors may possibly be the remains of a Middle Saxon church; part of the monastery established by Fursa and Foillan and given the name Cnobheresburgh.

In the late eighth century the East Anglian diocese was divided into two and a bishopric was created at North Elmham, in the north of Breckland. An Anglo-Saxon timber cathedral, the seat of the bishops of Elmham from c.672, was constructed on the spot now occupied by the remains of a Norman chapel and small castle.

Twenty or so of Norfolk's churches pre-date the ninth-century Viking invasions, including Loddon, Holy Trinity. Their early dates are indicated by dedications to saints such as Ethelbert, Withburga and Botolph. Situated near the east coast, the village of Reedham has one of the earliest known churches, founded in the seventh century by St Felix, who was the first Bishop of East Anglia. That period also saw the construction of other religious sites.

By the end of the seventh century monasteries were being founded, although physical evidence for them was largely removed during the period of the later Danish Conquest. Withburga (d. 743) founded a monastery at East Dereham.

Another was St Benet's, located on the River Bure, in 800. Elsewhere, a house for Benedictine nuns was founded in the parish of Outwell, at Molycourt Priory.

It was in the tenth century that the system of religious parishes originated. The ecclesiastical order established by the Anglo-Saxons centred around the establishment of minsters, or mother churches, with their own ecclesiastical territories, or *parochia*, which were based on earlier royal estates.

The return of Christianity also served to reintroduce literacy to England. Writing was to thrive from this time onwards, largely through the agency of the Church.

THE LAND

The small independent tribal kingdoms of the Middle Anglo-Saxon years steadily merged and had developed into large estates by the Late Anglo-Saxon period. The parish of Wymondham, which is the second largest in the county, is thought to be a rare example of a preserved large Anglo-Saxon estate. Most other such entities were subsequently broken down into smaller units and became parishes in their own right, with their own churches built by local lords.

Throughout those years there was steady and relentless clearance of native woodland. Some carefully managed islands of trees were maintained as a resource as wood was of primary importance for buildings in Norfolk in the absence of stone, as well as its many other uses.

Most of the population were engaged in subsistence farming. Cattle, sheep, pigs and goats were most commonly kept. Oxen were used for ploughing and pulling carts. Sheep farming increased in importance in the Late Anglo-Saxon period. The population grew wheat, barley and rye, together with peas, cabbages, parsnips and carrots. Agricultural innovation was driven by the developing system of lordship and centred around aristocratic and monastic sites. Careful land management resulted in improved farming methods and an increase in yields, which served to underpin the growing economic strength of the country.

In the far west, the Fenland formed a watery borderland, separating and protecting Norfolk and East Anglia from Mercia to the west. The land embracing the fen islands of the peat and silt fens had been occupied from early pre-historic times. Its population adapted most effectively to changing environmental and climatic conditions, with a lifestyle based on an understanding and control of the rich natural resources, especially the water meadows, which were most suitable for cattle grazing.

COMMERCE

The departure of the Romans in the early fifth century had caused disruption and a breakdown in commercial life. There was a cessation in the money supply and the use of coin for daily transactions was to cease for nearly another two centuries. It was not until the late sixth century that cultural and trading links were properly re-established with Europe and the Merovingian Franks, leading to the reintroduction of coins, with Merovingian gold issues, known as tremisses. The first English gold thrymsas were struck from around the 630s.

The earliest English silver pennies, today known as sceattas, were a development from gold coinage struck in northern Europe from the seventh century. As gold became increasingly scarce, more silver was used; a process that eventually resulted in an all-silver coinage, from about 660. The first East Anglian sceattas were probably minted in the reign of King Aldwulf (r. *c*.663–713). Sceattas are now being found in increasing numbers across Norfolk, indicating their importance in far-reaching trade and exchange networks. Far more common than later Anglo-Saxon coins, they circulated in greater volume and were probably used for everyday commercial transactions.

An extremely rare silver coin discovered at West Harling from the earliest issue of King Athelstan I of East Anglia (r.*c*.825–*c*.840) carries a rare depiction of a ship and reflects the region's international maritime contacts. It is evidence for trade with the Carolingian Empire and especially with Dorestadt (in the Netherlands), which was an important city connected with many international trade routes.

A mint was established in Norwich during the reign of King Aethelstan, King of England (r. 924–39). Coins are able to provide a record of some named people of that time, carrying the names of the moneyers engaged in their production. Those striking coin at Norwich at this time include people named as Bardel, Eadgar, Giongbald and Hrodgar.

The wealth of the area developed steadily, based on its agriculture, especially from sheep farming. Norfolk was an important centre for the production of wool even before the end of the Anglo-Saxon period. Other commodities were manufactured and traded, which included metalwork, glass and pottery. Pottery imports at Norwich indicate trade with the Midlands, the Rhineland and northern France.

THE ANGLO-SAXON ALPHABET

Although most of the population was illiterate, the Anglo-Saxons did have an alphabet. It comprised symbols known as runes, which were used from the fifth century onwards and until as late as the eleventh century in Norfolk. As well as forming a script, these symbols were believed to have a magical significance. An increasing number of objects inscribed with runic letters are being discovered in Norfolk.

One such item is a gaming piece formed from an ankle bone of a deer, discovered during excavations at the Anglo-Saxon cemetery at Caistor St Edmund in the 1930s, dating to around AD 400. It is inscribed with six runes, which spell *railhan*, meaning 'roe deer'. This is thought to be the earliest runic-inscribed object from England.

ART

Some astonishing works of art survive that provide us with insights into Anglo-Saxon society. One such object is a figurine known as Spong Man, which was found during the excavations at Spong Hill. It is a unique ceramic sculpture that depicts a figure seated on a chair in a pensive attitude. Spong Man is the earliest Anglo-Saxon three-dimensional figure ever found.

Excavations on the route of the Norwich southern bypass between 1989 and 1991 revealed another Anglo-Saxon cemetery at Harford Farm. One of the graves contained an elaborate disc brooch of the early seventh century, which had been battered and subsequently repaired before burial. It had been made from gold plate on a silver backing. The front is decorated with glass, ivory, shell, gold wire and garnets. In the centre of the backplate is a runic inscription that reads, 'Ludica repaired this brooch'. Through this personal inscription, Ludica has become the first Anglo-Saxon craftsperson whose name is known to us.

Another of the great discoveries of the period is a remarkable hoard of silver brooches, which was found in the churchyard at Pentney, west Norfolk, in 1977. They are some of the finest surviving pieces of Anglo-Saxon jewellery and clearly demonstrate both the wealth then available to aristocratic families in Norfolk and their access to silversmiths and craftworkers of the highest calibre. The hoard's burial date, thought to have been in the 840s, ties in with the first documented Viking raids on East Anglia, providing a reason for their burial.

VIKING NORFOLK

It was in the mid-to-late eighth century that the Vikings began to menace the north-eastern seaboard of Britain, in pursuit of loot and slaves. There was considerable impact on the native peasant population across the east of England, who were continually under threat of sudden violence and enslavement.

A 'Great Viking Army' arrived in 865 and took control of the major kingdoms of Northumbria and East Anglia. Under Ubba, they attacked Norfolk in 865 and established a base before moving on to attack York. The Anglo-Saxon Chronicle for the year 866 tells how, 'A great heathen army came into England and took up winter quarters in East Anglia. And there they were supplied with horses and the East Angles made peace with them.'

East Anglia had essentially remained independent to this point, under the rule of King Edmund (r. 855–69), the last independent Anglo-Saxon king of the East Angles. When they returned in 869, the Vikings took winter quarters in Thetford. Edmund fought the Danes in the vicinity of the town but was defeated, captured and killed. He is remembered today as Edmund the Martyr.

Following King Alfred's victory over the Viking chieftain Guthrum at the Battle of Edington in 878, the Danelaw was established and East Anglia became settled by the Vikings, coming fully under Scandinavian control. In the same year King Alfred made a treaty that formally gave East Anglia to Guthrum, who was subsequently baptised and christened with the name of Aethelstan. East Anglia remained a Viking kingdom, ruled over by Aethelstan until his death in 890.

When Danish settlers arrived in East Anglia, they adopted the native language. Archaeological evidence for Viking settlement in Norfolk is difficult to detect as their buildings have not survived. The extent of Scandinavian presence can be gauged to some extent by the use of their place names, specifically those coupling a Scandinavian name with an ending *–by* (meaning farm or village). Such names are most prevalent in east Norfolk. They are especially common in the far east, centred around Flegg and the hinterland of Great Yarmouth, such as Ormsby, Filby, Hemsby, Scratby and Thrigby.

There are also places that coupled Scandinavian personal names with the old English ending *–ton* (meaning village), as at Grimston. There is another group of Scandinavian-derived names ending in *–thorpe*. These are more widespread across Norfolk, although there is a concentration in the Tas Valley, south of Norwich.

It was during the tenth century, when Viking raids reached their height, that Thetford's role as a regional production centre developed at the expense of Ipswich, which was being affected by seaborne raids. Thetford became the main centre of pottery manufacture for the East Anglian Kingdom. The production of the ceramic known as Thetford ware, together with similar pottery types from Norwich, are indicators of the growing economic wealth and status of Norfolk at this time.

Buried hoards of Viking silver, usually containing metal ingots and 'hacksilver', have most often been found in the north and north-west of England, associated with intense Viking activity there in the tenth century. Now ingots of a similar type are being recognised in Norfolk, largely as single finds, demonstrating their widespread use in financial transactions in this area of the Danelaw. A hoard from Hindringham, in north-west Norfolk, is the first example of such hoarding activity in England outside of the North West and reiterates the continuation of Scandinavian practices in the county at this date.

LIFE IN VIKING NORFOLK

There has been much controversy over the nature of Viking presence in Norfolk during the years following the death of King Edmund. The Vikings were undoubtedly a violent presence across much of Britain but in East Anglia they did also show a keenness to integrate with the local population. Evidence from Norfolk suggests that the Danish warriors settled peacefully here. The invaders converted to Christianity and also adopted the native language. Archaeological discoveries have provided evidence in the form of metalwork items that reflect their lifestyle. Their material objects do not suggest much wealth or ostentation; mainly comprising household equipment and horse trappings that reveal the population had become one of mainly modest farmers.

The Vikings were enthusiastic traders and some of the coins that they used are evidence for their contacts with peoples right across the Viking world. *Dirhams*, which are Islamic coins, are known from across Norfolk and were used in currency across the Mediterranean world and the Byzantine Empire between the tenth and twelfth centuries. They reflect the region's role within a wider trading system.

It is perhaps ironic that by the end of the ninth century, just thirty years after putting him to death, the Viking settlers were using coins struck in memory of the deceased King Edmund, which are known as St Edmund Memorial Pennies. These may have been struck at Thetford, where there was a known mint at the time.

VIKING BELIEF

The first generation of Viking settlers were pagan. Burials of the period often contained personal possessions of the deceased, as revealed in a ninth-century double grave excavated at nearby Santon Downham (Suffolk) and in a single male burial at Harling.

Evidence for their pre-Christian beliefs comes in the form of Scandinavian-type objects, including a form of amulet known as the 'Thor's hammer'. These miniature charms were fashioned in the shape of the hammer used by the Norse god Thor and worn around the neck for good luck. More Thor's hammers have been found in Norfolk than anywhere else in the country and comprise another form of evidence that reflects the extent of the early Viking presence in the county.

In 918, the kingdom became absorbed into the West Saxon 'English' state under the descendants of King Alfred the Great. The resulting conversion of the Vikings to Christianity led to a Christian renaissance. Bishops of East Anglia were appointed during the tenth century and many new churches were built during the tenth and early eleventh centuries.

NORFOLK AND THE UNIFICATION OF ENGLAND

In 903 the East Anglian Danes waged war on Edward the Elder (r. 899–924), son of Alfred the Great and King of Wessex. Following a series of military defeats, East Anglia submitted to Edward in 918. In 927 Aethelstan united the Anglo-Saxon Heptarchy into the Kingdom of England. In the late tenth century Viking raiding along the east coast of England began once again. Records tell that both Norwich and Thetford were attacked and burned in 1004 by the Viking King Swein Forkbeard. After defeating the Anglo-Saxon ealdorman Ulfketel in battle at Ringmere, near Thetford, Swein ravaged the town once again. In 1016 Cnut of Denmark became King of all England. In 1017 Norfolk and Suffolk became the earldom of East Anglia under Thorkell.

Despite these political and military events, English agriculture and trade prospered. Economic activity thrived and an export trade in wool was developing with the Continent, which was to become so significant in Norfolk's medieval prosperity. By 1066, Norfolk had become England's most populous county, with a population of around 150,000.

In 1066 the Norse army under Harald Hardrada was defeated at the Battle of Stamford Bridge, near York. The same year then saw another foreign invasion that would have a profound influence on the development of Norfolk and its population. The impact is still to be seen today through its legacy of new buildings, art, towns and villages that created the fabric of medieval Norfolk.

5

THE NORMANS AND EARLY MEDIEVAL PERIOD

1066–1377

In 1066 England's army was defeated by invaders from across the English Channel under Duke William of Normandy, who subsequently became known as William the Conqueror. The Battle of Hastings was followed by the Norman Conquest of England. Another influx of peoples arrived in its wake from Europe and over subsequent years were to mix with the resident population.

William landed near the Roman fort of Pevensey in Sussex. Following the battle, he moved eastwards to Hastings (where there was a harbour) and then to Dover. Having secured a strong base, he moved west towards London, via Canterbury and Rochester. William then met with Anglo-Saxon leaders at Berkhamsted, who swore an oath to him. On Christmas Day 1066 he was crowned King William I (r. 1066–1087) at Westminster Abbey. England became part of the Anglo-Norman realm.

In direct contrast to the way in which England had previously been ruled, the country was now governed by force, with all power emanating from the king. William himself laid claim to vast areas of land, as well as granting tracts to his Norman barons in return for their military services and political backing.

The initial violent and bloody impact of the Norman Conquest quickly transitioned towards a period of stability and order. Under the new government, the Domesday Book provided a wealth of detailed information about the new kingdom. In 1086, when it was compiled, England's economy was essentially agrarian. The national population was about 1.75 million, of whom over 90 per cent lived in the countryside.

THE IMPACT OF THE CONQUEST IN NORFOLK

With the arrival of the Normans, Norfolk and England became part of an empire spanning the English Channel. As with the Romans and Saxons before them, the Normans introduced new cultural influences and heralded a new outward-looking era for the region. By the time of the Conquest, Norfolk had already become the richest and most populous part of England. The period has left a great visible legacy in the forms of many stone buildings, which remained as fixtures and symbols of religious belief and power throughout the following millennium.

The influx of people from abroad was not restricted to Normans. A French quarter was established in Norwich and a Jewish community arrived, representing around 200 people within Norwich's wider population of around 5,000. They settled between the market place and castle, which provided them with some security against a rising sentiment of anti-Semitism. It is with the Jewish communities of England that the earliest stone houses are associated.

In the medieval period we start to discover the names of more individuals and the roles they played in society, such as Isaac Jurnet, who was one of the Jews who arrived in the wake of the Conquest. He was a wealthy merchant and his house, which was constructed in the 1140s, survives under the Music House in Norwich's King Street, which was part of the thriving economic heart of the city adjacent to the river. It had an upper and lower floor, with vaulted cellars, and reflects the owner's wealth and importance.

King William confiscated the countywide holdings of the Saxon thegns and bestowed the earldom of East Anglia on Ralph de Gael (1040–96). After a Revolt of the Earls in 1075, Earl Ralph's estates were forfeited and passed to Roger Bigod, 2nd Earl of Norfolk (*c*.1144–1221). Roger was the son of Hugh, 1st Earl of Norfolk (1095–1177). The Bigod dynasty remained prominent in local and national affairs into the thirteenth century.

Norfolk's population continued to grow through the twelfth and thirteenth and into the early fourteenth century. Throughout that time, it remained the most densely populated and also the most intensively farmed region in England.

THE INTRODUCTION OF CASTLES

The Anglo-Saxons had built predominantly in timber. Their structures were relatively unsophisticated and have not survived above ground level today. When the Normans arrived, they made a massive and immediate impact on the landscape. They embarked on a programme of constructing large stone buildings, both religious (cathedrals, abbeys and churches) and secular (castles). The Jewish community played an important role in providing the funds for these projects.

In Normandy, castles were already widely used as fortified and defensible homes for members of the nobility and had become numerous during the early years of Duke William's rule. They were also centres from which estates could be administered and a strongpoint from which territory could be controlled. In the years following the Conquest, the Normans introduced castles to England, to impose their rule and their authority; siting them at strategic locations. The initial phase of their introduction was in the wooden motte and bailey form, which included the first castle at Norwich, which was possibly constructed as early as 1067.

The new skyline of Norwich would have been awe-inspiring to the population, with its huge castle, cathedral and church buildings. The castle, in particular, served as an imposing statement of Norman power, which was further enhanced by the impact of its construction, for which, according to the Domesday Book, 100 earlier Anglo-Saxon houses had been removed to accommodate the mighty structure.

The Normans often chose to position their castles at locations associated with earlier seats of power. Many were built within the decaying remains of Roman towns and sometimes prehistoric sites. Colchester in Essex is another East Anglian example, where the Norman castle was built on top of the Roman temple of Claudius. In Norfolk, early castles were built within the walls of the Roman fort at Burgh Castle, near Great Yarmouth, and in the south at Thetford, within the earthworks of a Late Iron Age enclosure, where a massive motte still remains prominent in the town. There was also a possible motte and bailey construction at King's Lynn, which seems to have been incorporated into later medieval town defences during the late fifteenth century.

Norwich Castle had a colourful history and was involved in conflicts on three occasions between the eleventh and early thirteenth centuries. The first involved the story of the Lady Emma de Guader (*c*.1059–*c*.1096), who held the castle when under siege during a rebellion against the Crown under her husband Ralph de Guader (*c*.1042–*c*.1096), Earl of Norfolk, in 1075. Emma led the defence of the castle, which was still a timber and earthwork construction at that time, for three months before surrendering to the forces of King William and managing to negotiate a safe passage abroad to re-join her husband.

As the Normans tightened their control across the country, they started a programme of building their castles in stone. William's close supporters were able to secure their positions across the land by the construction of thick-walled fortifications. Early stone castles were constructed at a number of locations in Norfolk. Their principal defensive feature was a keep, which is a large square or sometimes round free-standing stone tower in which the king or the leading nobles resided.

The importance of Norfolk and Norwich at this time are indicated by the construction of the elaborate new stone castle at Norwich, which was begun in *c*.1080 under King William II (r. 1087–1100). It was completed in *c*.1120 under King Henry I (r. 1100–35). The aesthetic appearance of castles was not normally a principal consideration. Their design tended to be functional but Norwich proved to be an exception. Its design was radical for its time and encompassed bold decorative architectural features not seen before, nor subsequently copied in other castles. Its external blind arcading and internal kitchen were innovative concepts. Norwich Castle has been described as 'architecturally the most ambitious secular building of its day in western Europe'.

Norwich Castle also has the largest motte by surface area in the country. This was a royal castle and continued to play a role in national events. During the reign of King John (r. 1199–1216), it fell to Prince Louis of France, evidence of which can still be seen in the walls which were breached and scorched by fire.

The Norman Empire wasn't confined to England and continued to extend across Normandy, where shared architectural influences are apparent. Elements of the plan and construction of Norwich Castle were subsequently used elsewhere and can be seen not only in England, as at Canterbury, but also in France at Falaise. More locally, Castle Rising, near King's Lynn, shares features of its design. Rising was constructed from *c.*1140 by William d'Albini, who in 1138 married Adeliza of Louvain (*c.*1103–51), previously the second wife of King Henry I, under whom Norwich Castle had been completed. That the design of Rising drew heavily on that of Norwich was, no doubt, through the influence of Adeliza.

At the same time, William d'Albini was building a castle at Buckenham in South Norfolk. The first castle there was a ditched fortification with an outer and inner bailey. In the 1140s d'Albini began work on another castle further to the south-east, subsequently known as New Buckenham. This construction contains a more unusual circular stone keep, within a circular earthwork.

Another motte and bailey was constructed at Mileham, in Breckland, prior to the 1140s, possibly by the Fitz-Alan family. It was situated on an important road linking the east and west of the county. The motte was protected by earthworks, with two crescentic outer baileys on the north side. The stone keep was square in shape. Its earth-works and central masonry survive well today.

Also in Breckland, Castle Acre was founded by William de Warenne in 1088. The higher part of the site was fortified with a rampart, ditch and palisade around a stone-fortified house. Outer earthworks extended down to the River Nar, which is believed to have been navigable and crossed at this point by the Peddars Way.

Tantalisingly, we know of a castle at Great Yarmouth that doesn't survive today. It was in use before 1209 and formed an important part of the town's defences. It stood in a location that is still called 'Castle Row'. This is thought to have been a simple construction, comprising a square keep with corner towers.

TOWN DEVELOPMENT AND SETTLEMENTS

The main period of town development in England was in the twelfth and thirteenth centuries. Domesday Book pro-vides us with a snapshot view of Norfolk towns in 1086 that helps us to understand their early growth. Burgesses were townsmen who had to pay annual taxes to the king. In that year there were 665 burgesses recorded in Norwich, 720 in Thetford and seventy in Great Yarmouth, indicating their relative sizes. A degree of planning in both Norwich and Yarmouth served to further assist their development.

Norwich was becoming the main town for the wider region, enhanced by its international connections, espe-cially with France, the Low Countries and Scandinavia. Accordingly, it was the natural place for a royal castle to be built. The stone castle and cathedral were conceived and developed together, which was a common pairing under the Normans. It became a prosperous international port and developed into a cosmopolitan city, stimulated by the commercial role of the thriving Jewish community.

At the time of the Conquest, Thetford was still the sixth largest town in the country. Domesday Book records that it had twelve churches and one monastery, together with its castle. In 1071 the seat of the bishops was moved there from North Elmham, but in turn was moved to Norwich in 1094. Thetford began to decline in the later years of the eleventh century.

The settlement at Yarmouth had developed from the early fishing community and became firmly established during the late Anglo-Saxon period. Its growth had been rapid; developing into a town within a single generation. The Caen stone imported from Normandy used in the construction of Norwich Castle and Cathedral was imported through the town. It was then trans-shipped to smaller vessels and sent by river to the city. Like Norwich, Yarmouth was another cosmopolitan town, attracting residents and merchants from all over Europe.

Each fisherman at the town occupied a strip of land, including a section of foreshore and higher ground where the house was built. There were narrow lanes between the strips allowing access between the river and beach. These narrow passageways, which became known as the Rows, were developing before 1100. Their layout can still be seen in Yarmouth's street plan today.

The early town was well defended. It was almost completely surrounded by water and connected to the mainland by a single causeway in the north. It grew rapidly and the port flourished. Domesday Book records Yarmouth in 1086 as a small but vibrant settlement, with a single church and population of around 400. It obtained a charter in 1208 under King John and the citizens were given freehold ownership of their lands. The town continued to expand until the middle of the fourteenth century. Its increasing prosperity was overwhelmingly centred on its herring fishing.

In 1262 Yarmouth was given a charter to build a town wall, although it took 111 years to complete the work. This was a massive undertaking and every resident was expected to commit to help for a number of days each year. Records tell how wealthy people would often pay others to do the work in their stead. When it was completed in the 1370s, no one was allowed to build outside and settlement remained within the walls for more than 400 years.

King's Lynn was another Norman new town, which was originally called Bishop's Lynn. Its importance grew as a result of its location on the Wash, on a sea route which facilitated North Sea trade. The town centre was constructed between tributaries of the River Ouse. The foundation has been attributed to Herbert Losinga, first Bishop of Norwich, although there was already occupation associated with a thriving salt-making industry around the Wash dating from Anglo-Saxon times and earlier. Losinga contributed a new church, St Margaret's, in the 1090s, which also served as a Benedictine priory. The town's Saturday market attracted traders from afar. Bishop's Lynn was given a charter by King John in 1204, granting some independence to traders.

Bishop's Lynn was another town with an early post-Conquest Jewish community. These people were tragically exterminated in 1189, during a nationwide outbreak of anti-Jewish expression and massacres.

Lynn was well positioned in relation to trade in produce from the Fenland and benefitted from a natural location ideal for the export of goods and well served by water transport. It had become a substantial trading port by the thirteenth century, handling a greater volume of trade than

London. It remained one of the country's richest ports throughout the medieval period.

Small towns and settlements grew up right across Norfolk. Some of these were created by manorial lords who were also building fortifications to safeguard their possessions. New Buckenham dates from the 1140s and 1150s, founded by William d'Albini (*c.*1109–76), south-east from his castle and the village at Old Buckenham. Albini also founded Castle Rising in west Norfolk, together with its castle. It has a planned street layout, associated with the late Norman church. Although now inland, it developed as a port on the River Babingley, which was originally navigable from the Wash.

The castle at Castle Acre was situated beside a planned town of the same name, adjacent to the River Nar. Its Cluniac Priory, like the castle, was founded by the Warenne family in the late eleventh century. The town was originally enclosed within a bank and ditch. Both priory and castle retain an impressive state of preservation today.

Despite the emergence of large and small towns, much of Norfolk's population remained scattered in smaller dispersed clusters of buildings and farmsteads. Markets grew up across the county from the mid-twelfth to the mid-fourteenth century. Most developed from existing settlements, often associated with a church or manor house. The development of new markets slowed after 1350.

Land handed to a Baron by the King was known as a manor. The manor was administered under the control of the Baron. Many of the French Barons chose to build castles on their land, while some preferred to build large manor houses. Norfolk villages were administered by the manors and often by more than one. Early manor houses tended to be sited near to the church. Moats started to be dug around some of the grander houses and agricultural buildings between the mid-twelfth and early fourteenth century, which tend to reflect episodes of instability.

THE CHURCH IN EARLY MEDIEVAL NORFOLK

By the time of the Conquest, Christianity had become the spiritual focus of society, underpinning daily life. The Normans' programme of constructing religious buildings in stone left its mark on Norfolk's landscape, which has endured to the present day.

Herbert de Losinga (1050–1119) was the first Bishop of Norwich and founded Norwich Cathedral in 1096. He had been consecrated Bishop of Thetford in 1090–91. Losinga also founded the churches of St Margaret's at Lynn and St Nicholas at Yarmouth, as well as Norwich School. North Elmham was the principal seat of the bishops of East Anglia until 1071, when it was transferred to Thetford. Thereafter, Elmham remained an important ecclesiastical site and the bishop maintained a large estate there, which contained his chapel. Located on the site of the earlier Anglo-Saxon cathedral, the Norman chapel survives today.

Domesday Book Volume 2 ('The Little Domesday'), which covers Norfolk, Suffolk and Essex, mentions 217 churches in the county. There were more medieval parish churches in Norfolk than in any other part of England at this time, together comprising the highest density of parish churches anywhere north of the Alps.

Many Norfolk villages had more than one church located in close proximity, including in the villages of Feltwell, Wood Norton, North Burlingham and Swainsthorpe. At the Burnhams, there were nine churches in the thirteenth century. Until the sixteenth century

Reepham had three, representing their adjoining parishes, but located immediately adjacent to each other within one churchyard.

Round towers are a feature of many East Anglian churches. The largest numbers appear in Norfolk, particularly in the south-east of the county. There are 144 recorded examples, of which a remarkable 123 remain standing. Their construction outnumbered that of conventional square towers in the eleventh and twelfth centuries. Just one other region in Europe, in northern Germany, has similar towers, which suggests enduring cultural ties between Norfolk and countries bordering the North Sea and the Baltic.

The centuries following the Norman Conquest were to be the main era of founding monastic houses. The programme of building Norman monasteries was based on the existing network of Anglo-Saxon minsters. All of the four main orders of friars, comprising the Blackfriars, Whitefriars, Austin Friars and Greyfriars, were represented in Norwich. The Greyfriars, or Franciscans, settled there in 1226. Benedictine monasteries were founded at Binham in *c.*1091 and in Norwich in 1096, where Herbert de Losinga founded a cathedral as well as a monastery. Others were founded at Horsham St Faith in 1105–06 and at Wymondham, by William d'Albini, in 1107. There was a single Benedictine house for nuns at Carrow, under King Stephen in 1146. One in ten of all monastic foundations in England between 1066 and 1200 took place within the diocese of Norwich.

Cluniac houses were founded at Castle Acre, Bromholme and Thetford. From the early twelfth century, Augustinian houses were constructed at Westacre, Walsingham, Creake and Weybourne. Castle Acre priory, together with Binham priory, today remain as important examples of regionally distinctive ecclesiastical architecture.

There were just six nunneries. In addition to Carrow, others were at Thetford, Blackburgh, Marham, Shouldham and Crabhouse. The last four were founded at rural locations, all in the Nar Valley of west Norfolk.

During the thirteenth century, orders of friars began to arrive in England. The Dominicans founded a house in Norwich. The Franciscans founded others on King Street in Norwich, Yarmouth, Lynn and Walsingham. The Carmelites established one at Whitefriars, Norwich, with others at Lynn, Yarmouth and Blakeney. The Austin Friars arrived in England in 1349 and established houses in Norwich, Lynn, Yarmouth and Thetford.

Small lead seal-like objects known as *papal bullae* continue to be found across the county, which attest the level of communication that was maintained with the religious government in Rome. *Bullae* were employed to authenticate papal documents. The density of Norfolk's parish churches and other religious houses meant that there was a continual traffic of both churchmen and directives from Rome. This was compounded by the presence of many Italians serving as ecclesiastics in the diocese.

The Church encouraged pilgrimages across medieval Europe whereby people could achieve salvation through visits to holy shrines. Pilgrims would band together and travel recognised safe routes, along which they would stop at cathedrals and shrines to worship saints and pay homage to religious relics. In England, Norfolk's Great Walsingham was such a destination, where in 1061 the Lady Richeldis received visions of the Virgin Mary. Walsingham subsequently became a shrine to the Blessed Virgin and an Augustan Priory was constructed around it, completed in 1153. Walsingham subsequently became a focus of worship for thousands of pilgrims from across Europe.

The county had a second destination of national renown at Bromholm Priory, which was situated in the parish of Bacton on the north-east coast. Founded in 1113 by William de Glanville, it was a daughter house to the Cluniac monastery at Castle Acre. This monastery acquired a fragment of the True Cross early in the thirteenth century, which made this a destination for pilgrims.

THE COUNTRYSIDE

At the time of the Norman Conquest most people were engaged in agriculture, which underpinned Norfolk's growing wealth and status throughout the medieval period. Fortunes were made, especially through sheep farming and the production of wool. Farming was essentially undertaken by peasants, who worked small-scale holdings. There was increasing pressure on available land throughout the eleventh and twelfth centuries, when marginal and wasteland were also taken into cultivation. Agricultural practices steadily became more intensive and an early form of crop rotation was introduced.

The growth in population, together with the shortage of land for both cultivation and pasture, resulted in the development of a new form of village layout where farmsteads were arranged around a green, which became common pastureland. This arrangement can still be seen in surviving examples, including those at Brisley, Hales and Mulbarton. By the end of the thirteenth century, twice as many villages and hamlets were centred around greens as along streets.

Open fields were a common sight right across the county. These comprised arable land divided into furlongs or blocks, which were then subdivided into smaller strips for cultivation. Grassland and hay meadows were also an important part of the farming landscape. The keeping of sheep and wool production continued to grow in importance, which led to the ongoing need for even more land for pasture.

Many villages shifted from their original locations, from the twelfth century and through the thirteenth and fourteenth centuries, with early examples including Longham and Mileham in central Norfolk. This process is evidenced by the locations of many rural churches, which today are seen rather oddly positioned as isolated monuments, away from villages and centres of population.

Almost all native woodland had disappeared from Norfolk by the time of the Conquest. Domesday Book lists a number of woods maintained for economic purposes on the heavier soils. In the absence of building stone, there was a huge demand for wood. Local woods were exploited heavily but there was still a need for soft wood, which was imported from Scandinavia and the Baltic, via Yarmouth and Lynn, from as early as the thirteenth century.

In the period following the Conquest, there was an increasing need for fuel, which was generally provided by timber. In east Norfolk, however, peat was used and became an important resource for the towns of Norwich and Great Yarmouth. The deep deposits in and around the valleys of the eastern rivers were steadily dug out but the resource was over-exploited. By the fourteenth century, and due to sea level changes, the workings flooded and the watery Broadland landscape was formed, which now characterises east Norfolk. A system of marshes, fens, rivers and lakes developed, forming the beautiful and unique landscape we know today. Surprisingly, it is only as recently as the 1950s, through the work of Dr Joyce Lambert (1916–2005), a native of Brundall, that it has been appreciated how the Broads were a man-made phenomenon.

An early form of map, which is held at the Norfolk Archive Centre, shows the extent to which east Norfolk has transformed; depicting the area as it was in about AD 1000. Known as the Hutch Map, it was made from a sheepskin and was created in the late 1500s. It portrays Yarmouth as a yellow sandbank in the mouth of the Great Estuary. By contrast, the mainland is shown as a fertile green area, intersected by the rivers Yare, Thurne and Waveney; all flowing into the sea. The region of Flegg, to the north, was a large island while Lothingland, to the south, formed a long peninsula.

The Norman period saw the introduction of some familiar animal species. Venison was a favoured part of the diet of the wealthy throughout medieval England. Although red deer were already present in the country, fallow deer were a Norman introduction. Most of Norfolk's hunting parks were created between 1100 and 1350 and over sixty have been identified; where a combination of woodland and grass were set aside for hunting and breeding deer. Rabbits were also introduced by the Normans and were prized for their fur and meat.

TRADE AND COMMERCE

The Domesday survey allowed William I to assess the wealth and assets of his new kingdom in order for him to raise taxes towards the needs of his administration. It has served to provide us with fine detail from which we too can understand the status of the country and the agrarian economy.

The economy of Norman Norwich continued to expand as a result of the more extensive communications established during the period. Caen Stone was imported from Normandy and was used in the more prominent buildings. A channel from the River Wensum into Norwich Cathedral Close was used to convey the imported stone, which was employed in the construction of the cathedral and castle.

Guilds of crafts workers were being formed by the thirteenth century, including those for drapers, mercers, wool sorters, weavers and dyers. The Guilds also set and enforced quality standards for cloth making. Through this process, Norwich maintained a reputation for the production of high-quality fine cloth.

The growing importance of the textile industry was facilitated by the role of Norfolk's coastal ports from where wool was exported to Europe and the Baltic states. Small ports grew up around the coast, notably from Cromer westwards, located on natural sheltered inlets. By the thirteenth century Blakeney Haven in the north, comprising Blakeney, Cley and Wiveton, collectively known as the Glaven ports, had become one of the major ports in the whole country. It had a particular strategic importance providing the sole safe anchorage between King's Lynn and Great Yarmouth. Trade and commerce thrived from there right through the medieval period.

Both herrings and peat were valuable to the medieval economy and Great Yarmouth and its hinterland was important in the production of both. Peat was dug across the region in the early medieval years and provided a major source of fuel across eastern Norfolk until the fourteenth century.

In relation to craft production, by the late Anglo-Saxon period pottery manufacture had spread beyond the towns of Norwich and Thetford into the countryside. One distinctive form of green-glazed pottery is known as Grimston Ware, which was produced in north-west Norfolk between the twelfth and fourteenth centuries.

Despite the many changes in the political administration, there was no significant change in the English coinage under the Normans. The established system of checks, controls and periodic changes to the coin types continued as before. The mint of Norwich continued to strike for all of the Angevin and Plantagenet kings, through to 1272. Thetford struck coin through to the reign of Henry II (r. 1154–89). There was also a brief period of coin production at Lynn under King John.

In 1241 the German cities of Hamburg and Lubeck united to establish a trading alliance that became known as the Hanseatic League. It was King's Lynn that was the key British link to the League and thus to North Sea and Baltic trade. The League was a trading network that extended right across northern Europe between the thirteenth and seventeenth centuries and brought prosperity to a large swathe of north-west Europe. It has sometimes been likened to a forerunner of the European Common Market. This was a powerful alliance of towns and merchants, created for the purpose of achieving the efficient movement of traded goods, and which operated largely independently of governments and political events. Members made tariff agreements and provided port facilities, while merchants used a common currency, language and legal system; adhering to common rules. Its success was based on trust in the systems and standards achieved.

Lynn was one of just three ports in England that were part of the Hanseatic League. The town's situation on the Wash, with associated river and waterway communications, made the port ideally positioned to join the network. By 1300 it had become a thriving international trading port exporting wool, cloth, salt, corn and fish, especially herring. Its imports included Icelandic fish, Russian furs and wine from Gascony. It also traded with other parts of England. The town has the only remaining Hanseatic warehouse in England, which was built in the 1480s.

LATER HISTORICAL EVENTS

Following the death of King Henry I, the period from 1135 to 1153 is known as The Anarchy, which saw the country reduced to bitter civil war. The eleventh century also saw the start of the Crusades. English participation was principally during the later twelfth century under the Plantagenet kings, particularly Henry II (r. 1154–89) and his son Richard I (r. 1189–99). In 1266 the episode known as the Second Baron's War, which was another civil war between a number of powerful barons and King Henry III, saw Norwich sacked and plundered by the defeated supporters of Simon de Montfort. From c.1290 onwards, England was constantly in a state of war. The Hundred Years' War started in 1337.

In the later thirteenth century Norwich, Yarmouth and Lynn all embarked on the construction of their own stone defensive walls. The reason was two-fold. Ostensibly it was to counter the threat of invasion from France but in reality it was also to provide an overt open expression of urban pride and wealth.

Norwich's walls were built between 1297 and 1344. They formed the longest circuit of urban defences anywhere in the country and embraced forty flint towers, twelve gateways and a brick and flint artillery tower, known as Cow Tower, was added in 1398–99. This formidable barrier provided not only a strong defence against any possible attack but also served to regulate trade and facilitate taxation.

Great Yarmouth was involved in long-running disputes with a number of other towns. Disagreements developed with Norwich and Lowestoft but the bloodiest confrontation was with the group of ports in Kent and Sussex known as the Cinque Ports. In 1297 the men of Great Yarmouth fought a pitched sea battle with those from the Cinque Ports in which twenty-five ships were sunk and 200 men killed. The tension between these port towns increased further still as Great Yarmouth's wealth increased and the conflict began to threaten the safety of the kingdom. Eventually the Cinque Ports began to silt up and their power declined, while that of Great Yarmouth continued to rise. In 1340 England defeated the French fleet at the Battle of Sluys. By that time Great Yarmouth was able to provide the king with more ships than all of the Cinque Ports put together. Admiral Pereborne, the commander of the English fleet, was also a Great Yarmouth man.

The mid-fourteenth century saw the first major outbreak of plague in Britain, later known as the 'Black Death'. Initially occurring in southern England and focused on seaports, it spread north and reached Norwich in 1349. King Edward III (r. 1327–77) and parliament attempted to maintain civil stability while the population fell by more than half, to just two and a half million, from the six million at the start of the century. In Norfolk, it caused a dramatic fall in agricultural production and in the overall level of trade. The effect on the economy of the major towns, Norwich and Great Yarmouth, was devastating. It also led to a large number of churches going out of use.

THE ARTS

The period following the Norman Conquest, with its continental influences, was a vibrant one for art and artistic developments. Norwich in particular had a strong artistic and craft community. The importance of the Church on society was strongly reflected in the art and material culture of the period and especially through its patronage.

The Normans introduced the Romanesque style of decoration, now most visible through their programme of constructing stone buildings. This new style was, in turn, influenced by native Anglo-Saxon and Viking art, as seen on decorative stonework, metalwork and sculpture. Norman stone buildings are distinctive for their rounded arches above windows and doorways, sometimes with decorative mouldings. Their structural interiors were supported by simple, heavy columns with decorated capitals. The churches of St Margaret at Hales and St Mary at Haddiscoe, both in south Norfolk, contain outstanding examples of elaborate early Norman decoration and sculpture. The new buildings would have appeared particularly striking in an area lacking its own building stone.

During this period of great constructions, it appears that most available resources were being used in the ambitious building programme, at the expense of other forms of craft production. From the date of the Norman Conquest until *c*.1200, there was a decline in the production of smaller items such as dress accessories, personal possessions and other portable objects, in comparison with preceding and succeeding centuries.

The late thirteenth and early fourteenth century saw a flowering of architectural sculpture. In Norwich, there was the construction of the cathedral cloister, with its famous bosses and corbels, and the rebuilding of the clerestory. Tomb sculptures and brasses were another form of early medieval high art. Surviving examples of important sculptural tombs can be found in the churches of St Mary and St Michael at Reepham and at the Holy Trinity, Ingham. An important early brass of Sir Hugh Hastings, from *c*.1347, survives at St Mary's church, Elsing.

The period from *c*.1300 to *c*.1360 was exceptional in terms of the arts across Norfolk. Books were being made in the Norwich area in the late thirteenth century. East Anglia was important for manuscript painting and Norwich itself was a major centre of production. The abbeys and religious houses were patrons for illuminated manuscripts, although the artists often worked from secular workshops across the region's main towns. This floruit of illumination lasted until *c*.1330. The culmination was the creation of some exceptional manuscripts including those known as the Gorleston Psalter, the Ormesby Psalter and the Macclesfield Psalter.

The Macclesfield Psalter, which is held at the Fitzwilliam Museum, Cambridge, is an outstanding example of medieval art, created between 1320 and 1330. It combines devotional imagery with depictions of everyday life. It is thought that it originated at Gorleston, south of Great Yarmouth, where it was possibly associated with the parish church of St Andrew. The manuscript depicts a range of animals, including exotic creatures such as apes, a lion and dragons. Marginal illustrations depict bizarre, humorous and even bawdy scenes, alongside religious imagery and another showing the process of medieval ploughing.

One particularly unusual and informative discovery from Norwich is an oyster shell palette, dating from *c.*1300. This humble object was found during excavations at the Norwich Greyfriars and provides an insight into the nature of the decoration of church interiors. Colour was an important feature of medieval architecture, although evidence for this has seldom survived. Oyster shells are not rare finds on medieval sites as oysters were a staple food. However, one particular shell was unusual in that it contained traces of pigment, having been used as a painter's palette. The inside of the shell contains pools of paint around the perimeter, including blue azurite, vermillion and black. Its use is most likely to have been to paint colour onto sculptural aspects of the church and serves to remind us that these historic buildings were once vibrant with architectural colour and figurative paintings, prior to the ravages of the Reformation.

6

LATE MEDIEVAL

1377–1485

Life in late medieval Norfolk, as with the whole of England, continued against a background of almost constant warfare. The Hundred Years' War against France lasted until 1453. Famous battles of that war include Poitiers (1356) and Agincourt (1415). The period also embraced the Wars of the Roses; the civil war between the Houses of York and Lancaster that culminated in the Battle of Bosworth Field (1485) and the defeat of the Plantagenet claim to the English throne.

Political instability and social unrest had been growing right across England through the fourteenth century. By the end, this had led to significant social change. The legal rights of peasants had grown and serfs were able to purchase their freedom.

We have a unique historical source for Norfolk, providing a lens through which we may observe aspects of English society and family life at this turbulent and lawless time. The Paston Letters, which were written between 1420 and 1503, provide a collection of over 1,000 papers and documents, unequalled in their importance, coverage and interest in relation to the life of an English family in the days before books were printed. The letters begin in 1420 through William Paston (b. 1378) and end with the death of his grandson Sir John Paston in 1503.

The Pastons were a prominent Norfolk landowning family, with properties including Gresham Castle in north Norfolk. The Paston Letters were not intentionally written as an historical record or diary but served the family's business purposes. Most relate to the period from 1460 to 1480 and were written by John Paston (son of William), his wife Margaret (c.1422–84) and their employees. The letters continued through other members of the family after John's death. Although much of the subject matter relates to the running of John's estates, they also reflect the lawless nature of the period and describe violent episodes when the Paston estates were subject to attack and seizure.

TOWNS AND SETTLEMENT

Norfolk in the fourteenth century was the most densely populated county in England. By the start of the fifteenth century Norwich had become England's second city and was reaching the pinnacle of its historic importance. Its walled centre was bigger than that of London. Wealth flowed from wool production and the making of cloth, and in 1404 the city received a charter from King Henry IV (r. 1399–1413). Its status is reflected in the grand Guildhall, with its flintwork façade, which was built from 1407 to 1413 for use by the city council and as a law court. Today, its extensive fifteenth-century features still survive, including an original doorway and stained glass windows.

Norwich's economic wealth was reflected in the many substantial mechants' houses, constructed above stone-built, brick-vaulted undercrofts, of which over sixty have survived. The most impressive is beneath the Bridewell (now home to the Museum of Norwich), which was built as a private house in *c*.1370, and became the Bridewell in 1585. Its stunning vaulted undercroft is accompanied by an exceptional knapped flint outer wall. Other undercrofts survive at Dragon Hall in King Street and Strangers Hall, which was a house owned by important mayors and merchants. The Strangers Hall undercroft is beneath the hall, which was built in the mid-fifteenth century for the merchant William Barley.

The city's continuing trading links served to add to its already multicultural population. Immigrants resided in enclaves close to the River Wensum. The wide variety of languages spoken in the city as a result was mirrored at the trading port of Great Yarmouth.

Yarmouth's prosperity was derived from the town's prominence as a trading centre. The most distinctive feature of medieval Yarmouth was its Rows; the narrow passageways connecting the quays with the main streets and Market Place. Some Rows were less than 6ft wide. They developed through the thirteenth and early fourteenth centuries and expanded in number with the booming herring industry through the fifteenth century. Most remained largely intact until as recently as the Second World War.

King's Lynn's trading had become more diversified by the late fourteenth century. The role of Dutch merchants enhanced its contacts with the Low Countries as well as the Baltic and North Sea. It traded with the cloth manufacturing centres at Bruges and Ghent and exported Norfolk's wool to them.

Lynn also enjoyed coastal trade with Newcastle and Scotland, importing coal, fish and hides. Exports included stone from Rutland and lead from Derbyshire. The town was eventually to compete with London, whose status continued to grow. As with Norwich, Lynn's prosperity is reflected in the construction of its Guildhall of the Holy Trinity, built between 1422 and 1428. It has a grand façade of flint and stone squares in a distinctive checkerboard pattern. This building houses what is considered to be the oldest theatre in Europe, with records telling of a young William Shakespeare appearing on the stage there in the 1580s.

FORTIFIED HOUSES

A new form of defensive dwelling developed at this time in the form of fortified manor houses, which reflect the unstable social situation and climate of violence, as revealed in the Paston Letters. They were also built as statements of power and prestige and some magnificent examples have survived to the present day.

Baconsthorpe Castle, situated near Holt, is a fine example of a fortified manor house. Constructed in the early years of the fifteenth century on the site of an earlier hall, it was associated with the prominent Heydon family. The almost square curtain wall sits within a moat, with towers projecting outwards. Later additions to the buildings include a long hall used for wool manufacture.

Caister Castle, situated just north of Great Yarmouth, was built between 1432 and 1445 by Sir John Fastolf. Grand in appearance, it comprised an inner and outer court, surrounded by a water-filled moat. Its ostentatious construction was financed through Fastolf's involvement in the wars with France under Kings Henry V and Henry VI. On Fastolf's death, the ownership was passed on to the Paston family. The castle was damaged when besieged by Sir William Yelverton, Duke of Norfolk, during a subsequent dispute over its ownership with John Paston.

The Paston Letters provide an account of how three of the family's manors were attacked and taken by force during these years. Caister Castle was taken, following the full-scale siege in 1469, and Hellesdon was also lost in 1465. The Paston manor at Gresham was attacked and taken in 1448 but was later recovered.

Another fortified house is at Oxborough Hall, in Breckland, south of Swaffham, which remains one of the best surviving manors of the period. It was constructed in 1482 by Sir Edmund Bedingfield. The Hall sits within a square moat. It retains a magnificent brick gatehouse, flanked by stair towers, which is an original feature. Oxborough has experienced a turbulent history, with partial destruction during the later Civil War, but has survived as the family home. Both Caister and Oxborough are characterised by their early brick construction. This reflects a continental influence, as well as the lack of good local building stone.

Other fortified buildings constructed during the fifteenth century survive at Dilham Hall, Elsing Hall and Middleton Gatehouse. As a group, the fortified houses perhaps have more in common with Norfolk's later grand country houses than with earlier medieval fortifications and in many ways they were precursors of the elaborate mansions of the mid-sixteenth century and beyond.

Another form of fortified building was constructed at North Elmham, which had been the location of the Anglo-Saxon timber cathedral. Although that role was moved to Thetford and subsequently to Norwich, North Elmham remained a seat of the bishops. Herbert de Losinga (d. 1119) had built a private chapel there. In response to social unrest and the Peasants' Revolt, in 1387 Bishop Henry Despencer obtained a licence to fortify the chapel. He added battlements and a half-turret to strengthen the gateway entrance.

THE LAND

At this time, Norfolk was the most intensively farmed region in England. The system of lordship and the role of manor houses were central to the way that farming was organised at a regional level. Within this system, peasants held their own land, while also providing services for the local lord.

Following the devastation of the Black Death, many communities were badly affected and suffered a fall in population. There was a resulting shortage of available labour and peasants were able for the first time to choose where they wanted to work. They experienced a period of improved legal rights and better wages, and this eventually led to workers becoming freemen.

Norfolk's flat natural landscape and fertile soils had always been well suited to sheep pasture and there was a further shift away from labour-intensive arable farming towards more sheep and wool production. Flocks increased, especially in the Fenland and large quantities of wool from there were exported through the port of Lynn.

Rabbits, which had been introduced to Britain by the Normans, became an important economic resource during the medieval period. Native to the Mediterranean, these creatures were naturally suited to the dry Breckland soils. They were most prolific in that part of East Anglia and rabbit warrens became a lucrative industry. During medieval times, their produce was considered a sign of luxury, both in terms of their fur and their meat. They started to be farmed for profit and many of the warrens were owned by monastic institutions. The rabbits were precious commodities and were held in enclosures for security and guarded by a warrener.

In *c.*1400 a very unusual building was constructed in Breckland by Thetford Priory, known as Thetford Warren Lodge. Essentially a fortified tower, it was intended as a house for gamekeepers and was also used as a hunting lodge for the Prior of Thetford. The building was subsequently used by warreners who farmed the rabbits.

The warrens remained a lucrative business until as recently as the nineteenth and even into the twentieth century. However, by the later years, rabbit products had lost their status as luxury items. Rabbits also lost their protected status in the 1880s and the use of warrens declined. The impact of myxomatosis in the 1950s eventually caused the rabbit population to decline significantly.

From around 1450 there was a shrinkage in rural settlement and a number of villages began to be deserted. Some of those affected had been established on marginal land but there were several contributory reasons. One was related to the social changes that had improved the rights of peasants, who were now free to move around and to seek better working opportunities and conditions elsewhere. Many villages had also been affected by the Black Death, with a subsequent decline in population. Soil deterioration, especially in areas such as Breckland, was another factor. The locations of many deserted settlements across the county show today as gentle earthworks, ditches and banks, which can be seen at locations including Pudding Norton, Roudham, Godwick and Houghton Park.

TRADE AND INDUSTRY

It was during the fourteenth century that the first Strangers settled in Norfolk. This name has been applied to groups of cloth workers from the Low Countries, who came to live in the county, arriving in two main waves. The first arrived during the fourteenth century and the second was to come later, in the sixteenth. These immigrants were highly skilled in the production of quality cloth and became associated with the village of Worstead. The wealth they generated can be seen reflected there in the scale of St Mary's church. The early Strangers also settled in Norwich, where they were initially greeted with an air of suspicion and some hostility, although they invigorated the city's cloth industry. A workers' hall was constructed at Norwich's Pottergate and dye for the cloth trade was sold at Maddermarket. Norfolk's wool and cloth trade was supported by an efficient system of water transport and network of coastal ports and harbours that provided access to the Continent.

A new merchant class emerged through the Guilds, who controlled trade in the larger towns, where they constructed their elaborate Guild Halls. This period saw Norfolk's position in relation to international trade bloom. A magnificent medieval merchant's house has survived at Dragon Hall in Norwich, which was built by Richard Toppes in the 1430s. A quay ran behind the hall, where trading ships would tie up to load and discharge cargoes. The riverside properties in Norwich were involved in the wool trade, which reached its peak in the fifteenth century, and the import and distribution of herrings. The city's prosperity was linked with the role of Great Yarmouth, to which it was linked by river transport.

Great Yarmouth was the site of one of the great medieval fairs. The Free Herring Fair lasted for forty days every year. It attracted merchants from all over Europe and the Middle East. They came to buy herring and trade in other goods. The fair grew as the fishing industry developed and in some years more than 350 ships paid the toll to trade there, providing great wealth to the town. Opening on the feast of Michaelmas, on 29 September, it began with a procession through the town.

Around the coast, villages and smaller ports derived a good living from the riches of the sea. North Norfolk's Glaven ports remained important, primarily as bases for longshore fishermen. Their catches grew in size and fish were salted and exported. Although principally engaged with fishing, some other products also passed through Blakeney Haven's ports, including salt, wine and local agricultural produce.

Communications by land in the later medieval period were also vital for the maintenance of trade. Local people were increasingly encouraged to use their profits from farming and commerce towards the upkeep of their roads and bridges.

RELIGION

The church continued to be the focus of medieval daily life. Norfolk's prosperity, derived from the wool trade, is reflected not only in the number of new churches but also in their size and sophistication. Their construction was financed by donations from farmers and merchants who had benefitted from the wool trade and who hoped to secure a place in Heaven through their visible philanthropy. Norfolk's 'wool churches' were massive structures, with tall towers. Prominent examples include those at Cawston, Salle, Ludham and Worstead.

This was the greatest period of church building, which marked East Anglia as distinctive, with the densest concentration of medieval churches anywhere in the Christian world. In terms of their architecture, there was a change to the Late Gothic, or Perpendicular, style in the later fourteenth century. Norfolk's churches of this period are characterised by their light, spacious interiors, as well as by the use of stone, which was imported through the port of Great Yarmouth. The Perpendicular style also combined the prominent use of wood for hammer beam roofs, rood screens, pulpits and benches. The construction of these churches embraced the wedding of faith, wealth and prosperity, together with artistic achievement.

HISTORICAL EVENTS

What was described as the Peasants' Revolt started in London and Kent in 1381, led by Wat Tyler, but there were many similar outbreaks across the country and violence subsequently occurred in Norfolk. The period of social unrest following the Black Death led to attempts by the wealthy landowners to undermine the improved conditions that had been won by peasants and to control their wages, through the introduction of the Statute of Labourers in 1351. Together with the introduction of the unpopular poll tax in 1377, the simmering civil unrest escalated.

Anger spread across society, involving not just the peasantry but also craftsmen, tenants, townspeople and even clergy. Violence ultimately erupted against those considered to be restricting wages and holding onto unfair feudal privileges. Rebellion broke out in Norfolk in June 1381, spreading initially through Thetford, south Norfolk and into the Fens. A group of rebels led by Geoffrey Litster moved north. Soon King's Lynn, Great Yarmouth and towns in between were involved. On 17 June a rebel force assembled at Mousehold Heath, to the north of Norwich, from where they entered the city.

In response, an army was assembled under Bishop Henry le Despenser. The opposing sides met on the 25th or 26th of June and fought a battle just to the south of North Walsham, in north-east Norfolk. The rebels were defeated and Litster captured. He was taken into the town, where he was hung, drawn and quartered.

The fourteenth century was a bloody one not only at home but also abroad. Sir John Fastolf (*c.*1378–1459) of Caister-on-Sea was an English knight who fought in many of the battles of the Hundred Years' War against France, through to 1440. He was initially a squire to Thomas Mowbray, Duke of Norfolk, before serving in northern France under Henry V. Injured in the siege of Harfleur, he missed the Battle of Agincourt, but later returned to France. Despite a distinguished and colourful military career, Fastolf is now better known to us through Shakespeare's timelessly popular character Falstaff, who was based on the Norfolk knight, and whose grand home was Caister Castle.

Sir Thomas Erpingham (*c.*1355–1428) was another English knight who gained national attention, both through his role as commander of King Henry V's archers at the Battle of Agincourt in 1415 and for his support of Kings Henry IV and Henry V. His name also lives on as a character immortalised in a Shakespearean play; this time *Henry V*. Erpingham's family held land at the village of the same name, north of Aylsham. He was a benefactor to the city of Norwich and one of the cathedral gates, which he funded in 1420, still bears his name.

THE ARTS

The county's general economic prosperity, expressed through the wealth of a number of individuals, gave rise to a strong patronage of the arts and a thriving artistic environment. The production of manuscripts and book illumination continued to flourish. Late medieval art was still predominantly religious in nature; a reflection of both the influence of the Church on society and also the large number of Norfolk churches. In Norwich alone, over thirty churches were built between *c.*1300 and 1500.

In terms of local craftsmanship, we can point to the media of stained glass and painting on rood screen panels as exceptional. High-quality stained glass of the period survives in the east window of the church of St Peter Mancroft in Norwich. Rood screens were wooden interventions in medieval churches that separated the chancel from the nave. Many were ornately decorated, with the use of fine tracery and carvings, although it is the application of paintings that distinguishes many outstanding examples in Norfolk. A large number exhibit painted decoration, depicting saints, prophets, other religious figures and biblical scenes. Most were produced during the fifteenth and early sixteenth century. Particularly wonderful polychrome figurative paintings survive on screens of the fifteenth century at Ranworth, together with other nearby Broadland churches at Ludham, Catfield, Barton Turf and Irstead.

Norfolk's strong tradition of writing goes back to the fourteenth century to the life of Julian of Norwich (1342–*c.*1429), who was the author of the first surviving book by a woman in the English language. Following a series of visions, Julian emerged from a serious illness and recorded her visions in *Revelations of Divine Love* (1395). She also wrote an exploration of their meaning in *The Long Text*

(1410s–1420s). St Julian's church stands adjacent to King Street, Norwich and, although gutted in an air raid in 1942, her cell and simple shrine can still be visited.

An important medieval manuscript in the form of a service book used by monks and priests is known as the Helmingham Breviary, which was made for use in the Diocese of Norwich and contains outstanding and rare forms of illustration. A record of 1422 tells of Brother Robert of Lakenham giving this 'new and great breviary' to the Priory of St Leonard's (which belonged to Norwich Cathedral Priory). Following the closure of St Leonard's Priory during the Dissolution of the Monasteries, it was held by the Tollemarche family, of Helmingham Hall, Suffolk, and has since been acquired by Norwich Castle Museum.

7

TUDORS TO THE EIGHTEENTH CENTURY

1485–1714

The 230 years covering the Tudors and Stuarts embrace the transition from medieval Norfolk to the early modern period. The age of the Tudors is often viewed as a golden age and a watershed in British history. The period starts with the accession of Henry VII (r. 1485–1509) to the throne of England, following the Wars of the Roses, ushering in the Tudor dynasty. It was dominated by the Reformation in England which was started in 1540 under King Henry VIII (r. 1509–47). This was a period of religious turmoil, with a series of events that saw the Church of England part from the Roman Catholic Church. It was to have a profound effect on the religious, economic, political and social development of the country. In 1603 King James VI of Scotland ascended to the English throne, ushering in the Stuart line. He became James I of England (r. 1603–25) and united the crowns of the two kingdoms. These years, through to the reign of Queen Anne (r. 1702–14), saw the throne held by queens on three occasions.

It was a time of strong economic growth, improvements in agriculture and an increase in the production and export of Norfolk wool. There was also a rise in foreign trade, with additional wealth arriving from the New World. At the same time, there was a growing gap between rich and poor and widening of social divisions.

This was an Age of Discovery, when European nations explored the globe. Colonies were established overseas and trading networks embraced the Americas and Asia.

There was a sense of wanting to understand the exotic world, of which snippets were brought back by seafarers. In 1607 the first permanent English colony in the Americas was founded at Jamestown in Virginia. There was also a renewed desire to examine the classical past.

The Tudor period was one of widespread social unrest, with a series of rebellions throughout the country. During the Stuart years, the great Civil War in England began in 1642, culminating in the execution of King Charles I (r. 1625–49) and the creation of the first Commonwealth (1649–60). This was followed by the Restoration of the monarchy under King Charles II (r. 1660–85). The union between England and Scotland was sealed in 1707. Both parliaments were united to become the Parliament of Great Britain, based at the Palace of Westminster in London.

England's navy and army were active throughout these restless years. During Elizabeth I's reign (r. 1558–1603), the Spanish Armada was defeated by the English fleet in 1588, during the period of hostility with Spain between 1585 and 1604. During the reign of Queen Anne, on land, the English defeated the French at the Battles of Blenheim (1704), Ramilles (1706) and Malplaquet (1709). Britain and France eventually signed the Treaty of Utrecht in 1713 to end the War of the Spanish Succession.

THE TUDOR COURT

During the Tudor years, Norfolk was faced with periods of civil unrest and also needed to enforce its own responses to religious changes, including the Dissolution, and to the disruptive political upheavals of the day. At the same time, a number of its citizens were directly involved in national events, through playing prominent roles at the Tudor Court.

Thomas Howard, 3rd Duke of Norfolk (1473–1554) was a leading politician during the reign of Henry VIII, as well as uncle of two of the King's wives; Anne Boleyn and Catherine Howard. Sir Richard Southwell (1502/3–64), High Sheriff of Norfolk, was a wealthy and powerful landowner with over thirty estates. He became a Privy Councillor and was involved in political events concerning the Tudor royal succession at several stages. Thomas Howard, 4th Duke of Norfolk (1436–1572), was a leading politician during the reign of Elizabeth I, to whom he was also a second cousin.

The Tudor royal family had other direct ties with the nobility of Norfolk. Queen Anne Boleyn (r. 1533–36) second wife of Henry VIII, was born and raised at the family home of Blickling Hall, in North Norfolk.

THE TOWNS

There was a great fire in Norwich in 1507, which removed much of the medieval city and many of the earlier buildings, apart from those built in stone, notably the churches. Through the scale of the reconstruction, it has sometimes been characterised as a Tudor city today, especially with the wonderfully preserved buildings in the vicinity of Elm Hill. The Dissolution also left a significant mark on the city, as elsewhere in the county. Among the religious institutions abolished were the Cathedral Priory, Carrow Priory and the city's friaries.

Throughout the sixteenth century Norwich was both the largest and the wealthiest city beyond London. It was a thriving centre for trade, although much of its wealth was restricted to the governing class, while the majority of the population lived in conditions of extreme poverty, which was becoming a national issue. The population doubled in the century after 1525 and parts of the city were subject to severe overcrowding, which was compounded by waves of Dutch and Walloon immigrants. Nevertheless, the city was considered progressive in its efforts to address the issue of provision for the poor, which paved the way for the later Elizabethan Poor Laws.

Queen Elizabeth I visited Norwich in August 1578 and stayed for almost a week. She resided in the Bishop's Palace in the Cathedral Close. During her stay she knighted the Mayor, Robert Wood.

Norwich continued to thrive in the seventeenth century. Its vibrant reputation was enhanced by its attractive range of buildings, shops and coffee houses. The textile industry was of principal importance throughout the sixteenth and seventeenth centuries, while associated trades proliferated. It was still also an important market centre for the region's agriculture. Increasing numbers of people continued to be drawn to the city and set up home in the expanding

suburbs, in turn putting more pressure on limited resources. Herring caught on the east coast were an important source of food for the urban population and they were regularly transported inland to the city by river from Yarmouth.

In 1536 the town of Lynn ceased to be under the protection of the Bishops of Norwich. King Henry VIII then claimed the town and what had been Bishop's Lynn became King's Lynn. It was home to wealthy merchants and there was considerable rebuilding between 1550 and 1650. Much of the new construction was in stone, brick and tile, replacing earlier timber. Cultural links with the Low Countries developed through trade are attested in Dutch gables, present on many of its buildings.

A notable building of this period is Thoresby College, which was founded in 1500 by the wealthy merchant and mayor Thomas Thoresby. The College was originally built for the use of priests and, at the Dissolution of the Monasteries, it was converted to a house and warehouses. This impressive building survives today, restored by the King's Lynn Preservation Trust.

Great Yarmouth was dependent on its quayside for the loading and unloading of ships. It was from as early as the mid-fourteenth century that the mouth of the River Yare started to silt up and threatened to become unusable. Over the next 300 years no fewer than seven attempts were made to construct a permanent outlet, or 'haven', but all of the early efforts silted up after just a few years. It was not until Joas Johnson, a Dutchman, was employed as engineer on the seventh haven that the problem was solved. Used to solving similar problems in Holland, between 1559 and 1567 he constructed the haven that is still in use today.

Although no traces remain today, Yarmouth still possessed a medieval castle at this time. We know that in 1550 it was transformed into a gaol. During the reign of Elizabeth I it was then used as a fire beacon. It was finally demolished in 1621 for building materials.

Thetford was a smaller town at this stage. It had many religious houses and was badly affected by the Dissolution, which caused a decline in economic and social life, leading to poverty and unemployment for the population. The main beneficiaries of the distribution of Thetford's monastic land were the Howard family. Another was Sir Richard Fulmerston, a minor government official and friend of the Duke of Norfolk. The town received a visit from Queen Elizabeth I in 1578 and also frequent visits from King James I (r. 1603–25) for the purpose of hunting; staying at his hunting lodge, which is now called 'King's House'.

In contrast to the fortunes of Norwich, King's Lynn and Great Yarmouth, Thetford's decline continued; lasting until the end of the eighteenth century. It retained some local importance as a regional market for south Norfolk, with an economy based on the woollen industry and clothing manufacture, together with sheep farming and rabbit breeding.

RELIGION

Monasticism in England came to an abrupt end between 1536 and 1540. All monasteries were dissolved under the authority of King Henry VIII. The Dissolution was set in place by Thomas Cromwell and Cardinal Wolsey and led to great changes in the religious landscape of the county. A series of anti-Catholic procedures were instituted through which Henry VIII disbanded Roman Catholic monasteries, priories, convents and friaries. Their estates were taken by the Crown and the land was then either sold or granted to favoured private individuals.

Very few churches were built in Norfolk after 1540. The Dissolution also led to a decline in pilgrimages. Great Walsingham suffered, having become a focus of worship for thousands of pilgrims from across Europe, and although Henry VIII himself had visited there twice, this tradition was curtailed during his reign. Bromholm Priory was also affected.

When Mary Tudor (r. 1553–58) became Queen she attempted to undo the Reformation put in place by her father and to restore the old Catholic religion. Her reign gave rise to a period of religious persecution. In Norwich, forty-eight local people were burnt, accused of heresy. One location for these executions is known as Lollards' Pit, located to the north-east of the city, where people were burned at the stake for their religious beliefs. Religious imagery was also returned to churches during Mary's reign, which included a new rood screen, depicting Christ on the Cross, at St Catherine's church, Ludham. The Reformation subsequently resumed on the accession of Queen Elizabeth I in 1558. Murals, statues, crucifixes and religious imagery were once again removed from churches. This programme was continued by the Puritans, under Oliver Cromwell, in the 1640s.

It was the dissolution of the Augustinian Priory at Beeston Regis, near Sheringham, in 1539 that led to the creation of Gresham's School at nearby Holt. The Priory had provided schooling and with its demise there was no remaining provision for education in the area. In 1555 Sir John Gresham founded a free grammar school, initially for forty boys. Today, Gresham's is one of the country's leading independent schools. Its alumni include W.H. Auden, Benjamin Britten, Ben Nicholson, James Dyson and Olivia Colman.

THE LANDSCAPE

During the seventeenth century Norfolk's landscape continued to be transformed by natural forces. In 1604, the sea eventually overwhelmed the small but thriving fishing village of Eccles-on-Sea, 12.5km to the north of Great Yarmouth. A storm removed great stretches of the eastern coastline and the village had to be abandoned. Its old round church tower survived as a monument to the town until 1895, when more gales eventually sent it crashing to the beach. In recent years evidence of this lost village has been revealed by wave action and many ancient artefacts recovered.

Norfolk's surviving ancient woodland was once again significantly reduced, between the years 1500 and 1800. Rare survivals from earlier centuries include Wayland Wood, south of Watton, and Foxley Wood in Breckland.

GRAND HOUSES

During the Tudor period the growth in trade, the redistribution of monastic wealth and the acquisition of land by both existing and new landowners led to an outward expression of their wealth in the form of new buildings. It was from around 1540 towards the end of Henry VIII's reign that a number of great houses started to be constructed and continued to be so for the remainder of the Tudor and Stuart years and beyond. Their development also saw villages starting to be displaced by large estates, associated with the houses, in the hands of new landlords. This further encroachment on existing villages and surrounding land, together with the removal of common land by enclosure, added to the tensions between social orders.

These great estates have left a legacy that characterises the Norfolk landscape today. Some of the earlier great houses, which date from the 1580s and '90s, include Breckles Hall, Costessey Hall, Flordon Hall, Heydon Hall and Dalling Hall. Others dating from the early decades of the seventeenth century include Barningham Hall, Kilverstone Hall, Kirstead Hall and Blickling Hall, near Aylsham.

Blickling had belonged to Sir John Fastolf of Caister during the fifteenth century and was acquired by the Boleyn family in the 1450s. Anne Boleyn, later to become the second wife of King Henry VIII and Queen of England between 1533 and 1536, was born there in 1507. The Hall that survives today was built over an earlier moated house by Sir Henry Hobart (*c*.1560–1625), the Lord Chief Justice. Blickling Hall was constructed in its present form between 1618 and 1629. The approach from the south has been described by Pevsner as one of the most spectacular in English architecture. Another fine Jacobean survival, Felbrigg Hall, close to Cromer, was constructed at the same time as Blickling, between 1621 and 1624, for John Windham (1558–1645). Felbrigg remains unaltered on the exterior and retains a fine Georgian interior.

Brickmaking had been reintroduced to East Anglia in the thirteenth century. However, it was under the Tudors that the use of brick really became fashionable and widely used. The grandeur of Tudor brickwork was manifested at several great houses including Thelveton, Kirstead, Salle and Heydon.

The proximity to northern Europe ensured that foreign building styles were adopted in the county. The Flemish bond became popular from the 1630s, which was a style of laying bricks head first (headers) and then lengthways (stretchers) in a single course. In the late seventeenth and early eighteenth centuries the distinctive brick Dutch gable was introduced. An earlier form is seen at Blickling and Raynham Halls.

A more local influence was the use of Norfolk reed for roofing. In the east of the county, reeds from the Broads were used for thatching, and there was one of the highest proportions of thatched roofs in the country.

AGRICULTURE AND THE COUNTRYSIDE

This was also the period when manorial lords began the enclosure of land, which was a result of the increasing emphasis on sheep farming and a process that was to continue through the seventeenth and eighteenth centuries. Enclosure removed the right of pasture enjoyed by small farmers, who until this time could graze their livestock on common land. The large landowners began to fence off and enclose the land for their own private use. The result on the countryside was an intensively farmed landscape, with the remaining open fields, which were divided into cultivated strips, interspersed with the self-contained enclosed farms in between. Large areas of the countryside were devoted to sheep grazing through the enclosure system.

The removal of the right of common pasture caused great anger and mistrust between the orders of society. However, the change did ultimately enable the land to be farmed more efficiently and facilitated the introduction of other new farming methods.

Alongside the process of enclosure, the period is associated with important agricultural innovation. Charles Townsend (1674–1738) is remembered for his contribution to what is sometimes called the British Agricultural

Revolution. Townsend was a Whig politician and brother-in-law of Robert Walpole. He became known as 'Turnip' Townsend for his interest in the cultivation of turnips, which alone was an important improvement to farming. Townsend also promoted crop rotation, made improvements to grasses and used marling, the application of a lime-rich mudstone, to improve the condition and fertility of soils. All of these improvements had a beneficial impact on agricultural production.

Agriculture in the Fens provided great wealth for west Norfolk and King's Lynn, through the farming of sheep, cattle and crops. The Fens were frequently flooded during the winter months. In the early seventeenth century it was appreciated that there would be advantages in introducing dykes and dams in order to provide proper drainage and improve the productivity of this naturally fertile landscape. Drainage of the southern peat fens was achieved once again through the county's association with the Low Countries, initially between 1630 and 1653 under the Dutch engineer Cornelius Vermuyden. The improvements continued through to the late seventeenth century, creating some of the best agricultural land in England.

The decline and desertion of villages, which had begun in the mid-fifteenth century, continued through the sixteenth and seventeenth. The process of the movement of villages away from their original location to beyond the boundaries of the new estates that were being created around the grand country houses is known as 'emparking'. Another cause of settlement decline at this time was related to the natural environment and the impact of coastal erosion, as seen by the loss of Eccles and other villages on the east coast, including Whimpwell, Keswick and Little Waxham.

HISTORICAL EVENTS UNDER THE TUDORS

The growing unrest within society led to a series of popular uprisings right across the country, with a number of movements against the authority of the Tudor monarchs. These extended from Yorkshire in the north, in 1486, to Cornwall in the south, in 1497, and Essex in 1601, towards the end of Elizabeth's reign. For a brief period in the mid-sixteenth century a local rebellion led by Robert Kett made Norfolk the focus of the whole country's attention.

At this turbulent time, the whole of East Anglia descended into civil unrest. Food prices were high and the gentry were hated by many people, particularly as a result of the enclosure process. With ongoing efforts to maximise the income possible from the wool trade, the enclosure of common land for sheep farming had become a major grievance right across southern England. People were fed up with common land being taken away from them. It was during the reign of King Edward VI (r. 1547–53) that simmering unrest ignited into a major popular uprising. Following a large gathering at Wymondham Fair, south of Norwich, in 1549 a group of local peasants proceeded to break down fences that had been erected around common land by John Hobart, Lord of the Manor at nearby Morley.

Robert Kett (1492–1549), a yeoman farmer and landowner at Wymondham, offered to lead the rebels in a protest, 'in defence of their common liberty'. Together, they marched towards Norwich, rallying with supporters beside an oak tree at Hethersett, to the north-east of Wymondham, on 9 July. The oak tree still survives and is a living memorial to Kett and his followers.

The rebels finally established a camp on Mousehold Heath, overlooking Norwich, where some 15,000 gathered. Over the following weeks there were a series of battles and for a while the rebels controlled the city. Successive royal armies were sent to deal with the troubles. Eventually, the rebels were engaged by the Earl of Warwick in a final battle at Dussindale, to the north-east of the city, on 27 August. Some 3,000 rebels died and a further 200 were captured and hanged outside the city's Magdalen Gate. Kett was later captured. He was imprisoned and finally executed outside Norwich Castle on 7 December.

This tragic and shockingly bloody episode had a national resonance at the time, although it is best remembered in Norfolk today. Kett's rebellion characterised the national struggle by the poor for rights against the greed and oppression of the wealthy. The stand made by Kett in the face of overwhelming odds has ensured his enduring memory as a local folk hero, alongside Queen Boudica and others still to enter the historical record.

NORFOLK AT WAR

Until the Tudor period Norfolk's defensive structures had mainly been situated inland. Castles had been constructed by local lords as symbols of power and authority, and to subjugate the population. It was a reflection of regal authority under the Tudors that internal private power struggles were reduced and the emphasis of national defence was focused outwards, at the coast.

During the years 1539–40 Henry VIII looked to secure the English coast in the face of threats from his main European rivals, the Emperor Charles V, Holy Roman Emperor and King of Spain, and Francois I, King of France, who might look to reclaim England for the Catholic Church. He constructed fortresses in southern counties and looked to identify key defensive locations on the Norfolk coastline. His main efforts were eventually concentrated on Norfolk's major ports, Great Yarmouth and King's Lynn, and which also included Blakeney harbour.

Under Elizabeth I, in 1588, a new threat came from the Spanish Armada. It was identified that King's Lynn, Weybourne and Yarmouth were in need of further strengthening. King's Lynn had already been provided with a fort at St Anne's. A small earthen fort was also constructed at Weybourne in the north. Cannon were then located at intervals along the coast. At Yarmouth the town wall was revetted with an earth bank.

LATER HISTORICAL EVENTS

Despite the undercurrent of civil unrest, the Tudors managed to unite the nation around the institution of the Crown. At the end of Elizabeth's reign, England was not in a position to rival the major powers of France and Spain but the country was at peace and was engaging in international affairs through trade. When Elizabeth died in 1603 she had no direct heir and requested that the Protestant James, son of Mary Queen of Scots, should succeed her. James I (r. 1603–25) became the first Stuart monarch and was in turn succeeded by Charles I (r. 1625–49), during whose reign the country was to descend into Civil War.

Norfolk remained comparatively peaceful during most of the English Civil War of 1642–48. At its outbreak there was a diversity of allegiance right across society, leaving many families divided. The county is associated with a strong support for Parliament but at the outset many of Norfolk's gentry supported the Royalist cause, while the majority of people in the area supported a moderate Puritanism. The active Puritans in the region were well organised and were able to mobilise the strongest local support and suppress the Royalist opposition.

Norfolk's allegiance to Parliament was maintained through its membership of the defensive alliance known as the Eastern Association, alongside Suffolk, Essex and Cambridgeshire. Thereafter, the area was unaffected by major battles. Norwich in particular was strongly Parliamentarian and the city was considered key to the defence of the county. The city walls had fallen into disrepair and £200 was provided for their restoration. They were also fortified with cannon. Norwich Castle was similarly refortified, for the last time in its long history. Booms were installed on the river at Norwich and a chain laid across the Yare at Great Yarmouth.

Whilst Norfolk overall was strongly committed to the Parliamentarian cause, the Royalists were aware of the key strategic importance of King's Lynn and its port in the west. Although Royalist support had been effectively suppressed across most of Norfolk, in August 1643 King's Lynn declared for the Crown. Parliamentary forces under the Earl of Manchester, assisted by Oliver Cromwell, laid siege to the town with 18,000 men. Lynn eventually fell to Manchester's army in September that year.

Some Royalist sympathy also existed further south, at Lowestoft, where supporters of the King converged in early March 1643. Oliver Cromwell, who was in Norwich at the time, set out with five troops of the Eastern Association and recovered the seaside town without bloodshed, leaving a cavalry detachment in the area. In 1989, a coin hoard of the period, buried in 1643, was discovered at Wortwell, in the Waveney Valley, close to the Suffolk border. The hoard was concealed in the ground, some 18 miles inland from Lowestoft, apparently by a Royalist sympathiser who had been targeted by

Cromwell's troops when they were raiding in the vicinity. After 1643 Norfolk remained a relatively peaceful area and there were few subsequent disturbances.

There were Norfolk individuals who remained loyal to the King. Sir Henry Bedingfield (1582–1657) was Sheriff of Norfolk and he, along with his sons, fought for the Royalists at Marston Moor in 1644. Sir Henry was later imprisoned in the Tower of London. His home at Oxborough Hall was ransacked and partly burned down. The house was rebuilt during the Restoration, under King Charles II, when the Bedingfield family found favour with the new King for their enduring loyalty to the throne and to the Catholic faith.

Norfolk was to make one more contribution to national events at the close of the Civil War. A bailiff of Great Yarmouth named John Carter had a house on South Quay. It was there in 1648 that the Parliamentarian leaders met and took the fateful decision that the King should be tried and executed. Now known as the Elizabethan House, Carter's home has been preserved as a memorial to this historic meeting.

THE LATER SEVENTEENTH CENTURY

The second half of the seventeenth century saw a new seaborne threat during the Anglo-Dutch wars, especially between 1652 and 1684. Hostilities had ignited between the nations through clashes over trading and overseas colonies. Militia were mobilised to guard strategic positions along the coast, especially the flat beaches to the north of Great Yarmouth and around Weybourne. Old signalling beacons erected at the time of the Armada were called back into use and a small brick fort was constructed by the river mouth at Yarmouth.

In 1685 King James II (r. 1685–88) raised eight new regiments to help quell the Monmouth Rebellion, which was an attempt to overthrow the new king in favour of the Duke of Monmouth, illegitimate son of Charles II. One of these was Colonel Henry Cornwall's Regiment of Foot, later known as the 9th Foot and to become the Royal Norfolk Regiment. The Regiment served with distinction in campaigns across Europe between the years 1689 and 1694. They served in Ireland and fought in actions including the Battle of the Boyne. They then participated in expeditions against France, which involved a dramatic raid on the port of Brest. From 1701 they fought in Europe during the War of the Spanish Succession.

TRADE AND INDUSTRY

By 1500 only about thirty-five markets remained in the county, from an earlier medieval peak of 138. While declining in number, some became larger. Swaffham, in central Norfolk, is an example of a medieval market that has become a permanent institution to this day.

The early sixteenth century had seen a decline in the wool trade. The Norwich textile industry was beginning to struggle because of changing public tastes and also from continental competition. In 1565 a new wave of Strangers arrived in Norwich to reinvigorate the industry. These Protestant refugees from the Spanish Netherlands were skilled workers and were invited to settle in the city. Thirty families arrived in 1565 and they subsequently developed into a substantial community. They introduced new advanced techniques and methods that stimulated the textile industry, through passing on their skills to the local population. The materials they produced were lighter and well-finished. Their produce included fine clothing and dresses, scarves and shawls. Norwich's prosperity steadily revived thereafter. When Queen Elizabeth I visited the city in 1578, she was impressed by the work of the Strangers, along with demonstrations of their spinning and weaving skills.

King's Lynn's trade and industry flourished under the Tudors. At the beginning of the seventeenth century the town was a thriving port of comparable size to Bristol. At this time its international trade routes encompassed Norway, Greenland, Iceland, the Baltic and Low Countries. Its coastal trade included the import of coal from Newcastle, while corn was its major export. Great Yarmouth also engaged in international trade with countries including Norway, Spain and Italy. In the north, the Glaven ports of Blakeney, Cley and Wiveton remained important for merchant shipping into the seventeenth century. Wells harbour also thrived from the late sixteenth century.

The unstable political situation from the 1630s caused financial difficulties and damage to trade and the running of the economy. There had been a reduction in the size of silver coins that, coupled with a shortage of small change in circulation, led to the need for a form of currency that would enable small monetary transactions. During the aftermath of the Civil War, tradespeople sought to address this need and started to produce their own versions of farthings, which we now call trade tokens.

These tokens were produced across the country between 1648 and 1672. They were issued by local traders, who gave them to customers as small change. People had to trust the traders, for if they went out of business, their tokens would become worthless. It was not only the tradespeople in the major towns of Norwich, King's Lynn and Great Yarmouth who issued tokens. Those from dozens of smaller villages also produced them. These tokens carry the names and professions of the traders, providing us with a wealth of information about specific individuals and their working lives.

NORFOLK WITHIN THE WIDER WORLD

It was at this time that Europeans set out to distant shores, not only to find new territories and fortunes but also in the quest for new knowledge. There were no public museums in seventeenth-century England and members of the nobility sought to form collections of items from abroad in order to reflect their own learning and status. A renowned collection was assembled by the Paston family, held at their home of Oxnead Hall. It contained pictures, sculptures and fine objects, reflecting what was considered to be the range of people's achievements.

The developing exploration and awareness of the world in the seventeenth century is expressed through a painting of the 1660s and '70s from their collection, known as the Paston Treasure, which is displayed at Norwich Castle Museum, and portrays part of their magnificent collection. The painting is unique in the history of British collecting as a depiction of a *schatzkammer*, or 'cabinet of wonders'. It was commissioned by Sir Robert Paston (1631–83); a prominent supporter of King Charles II. It depicts things from Europe, Asia, Africa and America; encompassing the known world of the mid-seventeenth century. Their diversity embraces Chinese porcelain, an African parrot and monkey, and Indian tortoiseshell, while the New World is represented by tobacco from Virginia. A young slave, himself a contemporary status symbol, is the earliest known portrait of an African in Norfolk. The picture is a reminder not only of contemporary aristocratic tastes but of a developing knowledge of the world in Norfolk 350 years ago.

Norfolk's links with North America are further revealed through the story of Pocahontas (*c.*1596–1617); a native American whose personal life became associated with the early colonial settlement at Jamestown, Virginia. The popular story of her life tells how she saved that of Englishman John Smith in 1607. She later converted to Christianity and married tobacco planter John Rolfe. Moving to England, the couple lived at their homes at Heacham Hall in northwest Norfolk, as well as London.

Back closer to Britain, events on the European mainland during this turbulent period resulted in the displacement of peoples, with families from abroad arriving in Norfolk and introducing new cultural influences. The Strangers themselves were Protestant refugees from the Spanish Netherlands. Other refugees arrived from France, where religious intolerance had surfaced in the 1680s. French Protestant families, known as the Huguenots, were forced to flee to England. Many of these refugees who settled in Norwich were skilled silk workers and readily integrated into the economic life of the city.

THE ARTS AND SCIENCE

The range of arts, together with progressive thinking and writing, were well served during the Tudor and Stuart years. In particular, contacts with the wider world provided a source of inspiration and ideas. The influences of Dutch and French incomers can be seen in the architecture of the seventeenth and eighteenth centuries. These new communities influenced local life in many ways. The Dutch even brought canaries with them, which to this day provide the adopted name of Norwich City Football Club.

The decades after 1500 had given rise to a scientific revolution, personified by the renowned thinker and academic Sir Thomas Browne (1605–82) who moved to Norwich in 1637. His diverse interests spanned the fields of science, medicine, religion, the natural world, history and antiquarianism. As a writer, his initial literary work, *Religio Medici*, was both provocative and influential. It was translated into a range of European languages.

A little known but important early history relating to the east of the county was written at this time by Henry Manship (b. 1555), who was a local schoolmaster and member of the town council. His *Booke of the Foundacion and Antiquitye of Great Yarmouthe* was meticulously researched from documents held not only locally but also at the Tower of London. His work remains an important historical source for the period between 1611 and 1619 in Norfolk.

The richness of the county's church rood screens was mentioned in the previous chapter. Norfolk and Suffolk are the main counties in England in which so many screens have survived the Reformation. Parts of over 200 wooden examples remain in Norfolk, although many of these have been damaged. For example, the exceptionally fine fifteenth-century panel paintings at All Saints' church, Catfield, remain largely intact but the faces of the saints and kings have been scratched and defaced.

8

THE HOUSE
OF HANOVER

1714–1837

When Queen Anne, the last Stuart monarch, died in 1714, the crown of England passed to her German cousins in the House of Hanover, as a result of the Act of Settlement. King George I (r. 1714–27) was initially unfamiliar with his new kingdom and its language and looked for close advisers. This provided an opportunity for the advancement of prominent Norfolk landowner Sir Robert Walpole (1676–1745), who became the country's most influential politician and was the first minister to be given the title of 'Prime Minister'.

As leader of the Whig Party, Walpole opposed foreign military interventions, which were to dominate political affairs and international relations from the later eighteenth century. He was also the first in the long line of Prime Ministers to inhabit what was originally considered to be the modest town house in Downing Street, situated close to the centre of government. Walpole remains Britain's longest serving Prime Minister, holding office for over twenty years, between 1721 and 1742.

This period has been characterised as a 'restless age' and an 'Age of Revolution'. The mid-eighteenth century saw a transformation in Britain, with the birth of the Industrial Revolution, hand-in-hand with rapid economic growth. It was also a period of warfare from the later years of the century, which included war with America and the Napoleonic Wars in Europe. During the early nineteenth century, Britain was to emerge as the principal global naval and imperial power.

At this time Norfolk's agricultural role came to national prominence, as a cradle of important innovation. Changes in the countryside were driven by the growth of the large country estates, which served to shape the subsequent development of the county in many ways. At the same time, some of Norfolk's citizens were to play prominent roles on the wider world stage, influencing international events.

NORFOLK'S TOWNS

There was a rapid rise in the population across England and Wales, from around five million at the start of the eighteenth century to over nine million in 1800. The eighteenth century saw improvements in the quality of town life as England was transformed from a rural nation into an essentially urban country. Major advances were made with the introduction of sewers and water mains were laid. Streets were cobbled and paved for the first time. Lighting of streets was introduced and there were attempts to control rubbish pollution.

At the start of the eighteenth century Norwich was England's largest provincial city. It was one of only five urban centres with a population of more than 10,000, along with York, Bristol, Exeter and Newcastle. Norwich was also acknowledged as a centre for the arts and fashion.

The appearance of the city underwent further transformation, both through necessity and through civic pride. Its walls needed to be repaired in 1727 and the gates were pulled down between 1790 and 1808. Additional housing was needed for workers drawn to the city and steadily grew up beyond the old walled area. More centrally, there was considerable investment in civic buildings, including the Octagon Chapel in 1756 and the Bethel Hospital in 1724. The Assembly Rooms were completed between 1754 and 1755 by Thomas Ivory and Sir James Burrough. Medieval earthworks that had been part of the castle bailey were levelled to provide space for a new cattle market in 1738.

The mid-eighteenth century was the golden age of the Norwich textile industry, when half of the city's population were involved in the production of cloth; an industry that also engaged much of the surrounding countryside. Its hand-weaving industry managed to compete with production in the industrialised north, through its highest quality handmade products in worsted and silk. New businesses also developed that reinvigorated the trade, the most important of which was the manufacture of Norwich shawls.

The shawl was a fashion garment that had originated in Kashmir, India. Their manufacture in Norwich began in the 1780s. The city led the way in producing shawls as soft as those from Kashmir. Shawls became a valued fashion item during the early nineteenth century. Norwich was also renowned for the quality of its dyeing. The colour red became associated with the city and known as 'Norwich Red'. By 1800 there were twenty shawl producers working in Norwich. The industry was a major employer and production was focused in the vicinity of the River Wensum. Other Norwich industries at this time were tanning, leatherworking, malting and brewing.

King's Lynn was still a thriving port town. The harbour was silting up by the eighteenth century and its port was canalised between 1798 and 1828 in order to drain waters into the Wash and a new quay was installed. The port was unequalled in its location for trade, situated on the Wash and at the mouth of the River Ouse. It continued to import coal from Northumberland and Durham and also wine from France, and exported these goods to London and other parts of England, as well as abroad. Fishing and whaling vessels used the port. Lynn maintained two weekly markets, which attracted people from far afield and gave rise to additional services as well as inns and a range of shops.

Great Yarmouth was the only secure anchorage on England's east coast for merchant vessels travelling between the Humber and Thames. It was a major naval base and active during the Napoleonic Wars. Nelson himself returned there following the battles of the Nile (1798) and Copenhagen (1807). In his tour through Great Britain between 1724 and 1726, the writer and traveller Daniel Defoe described Yarmouth as a beautiful town, situated in an ideal position for trade and with 'the finest quay in England, if not in Europe, not inferior even to that of Marseilles'. By the early eighteenth century the town certainly had many fine buildings, which included St George's Chapel (1714), the Custom House and the Fishermens' Hospital (1702). The Herring Fair continued to be held and the fish were exported to Italy, Spain, Portugal and Russia, as well as woollen and other products to Holland, Norway and the Baltic. During the eighteenth century Great Yarmouth also became a fashionable place to visit for tourism and as a watering place. The population of the town doubled during the first half of the nineteenth century.

On the north coast, the ports at Blakeney and Cley were beginning to fall behind the other large coastal ports during the earlier years of the eighteenth century. Their coastal channels and shallow harbour were silting up. Ships used for foreign trade were also getting larger and could no longer reach the quayside. Foreign trade was focused on the export of local grain. Salt was also produced at Cley, both for the county's use and for export, notably to Holland.

Daniel Defoe made special mention of Norfolk's market towns, which he described as being 'more and larger than any other part of England'. Dedicated market places were established at Swaffham, Dereham, North Walsham, Wymondham, Diss and Holt. Smaller market towns across the county still flourished, reflecting the prosperity of the period, including Acle, Thetford, Alysham, Reepham and Fakenham.

In north Norfolk, Holt had developed as a thriving market town, with its prosperity growing following the founding of Gresham's School. Today Holt provides us with a window into what a Norfolk Georgian town looked like. Following a major fire in 1708, the town was rebuilt and a new centre was created with rows of Georgian properties established, creating the outline appearance we see today.

SOCIAL WELFARE IN HANOVERIAN NORFOLK

Unemployment was becoming more of a social issue and problem across society. From as early as the mid-sixteenth century Acts had been passed to provide a degree of social provision, which were known as the 'Old Poor Law'. Money was collected from households to provide relief for the poor. It was at the end of the sixteenth century that the first workhouses were created. These were establishments in which people who could not support themselves were provided with accommodation and employment.

In 1723 the Workhouse Test Act was passed, through which anybody who wanted to receive poor relief had to enter a workhouse and undertake work there. These establishments were built across the country and in 1776 some twenty-four were recorded in Norfolk, situated mainly in the towns. By 1803 this had substantially increased to 130 across the county, which provided for 4,000 inmates.

RELIGION

Religious dissent had been steadily growing among the population. During the sixteenth and seventeenth centuries people began to move away from their previous adherence to the established Church. By the eighteenth century, although the Anglican Church still predominated, it was joined by those of nonconformists, Baptists, Methodists, Independents and Congregationalists. The later eighteenth century also saw the arrival of the Wesleyans.

Churches remained a dominant feature of the Norfolk landscape, although their distribution at this time still largely related to the pattern of earlier medieval settlement. The result was that Norfolk's large churches were set among what were becoming shrinking rural populations and, as a result, many of these great buildings were poorly maintained and were being left in disrepair.

The clergy at this time often needed to rely on additional means of income and few parishes were left with a resident vicar. The diaries of Parson Woodforde (1740–1803) provide a charming insight into the life of a country parson in Georgian Norfolk. James Woodforde was a clergyman in the Church of England. He lived a largely uneventful life but his diaries provide a delightful and detailed account of rural Norfolk. Woodforde lived at Weston Longville, north-west of Norwich. He described Norwich as 'the fairest city in England by far' and explained how much he enjoyed visiting the beach at Great Yarmouth.

AGRICULTURE AND THE LAND

The eighteenth and nineteenth centuries saw important advances in agriculture, with Norfolk playing a leading role in national developments. The period after 1720 experienced a steady growth in the population and Norfolk's farming was important in providing food for the nation.

Norfolk's larger landowners began to introduce important changes. The first was a new system of crop rotation that had been developed and used in the Low Countries, resulting in an increase in crop yields. The county's landowners were to recognise and adapt that practice, which became known as the 'Norfolk Four Course' system. This system became standard practice on British farms during the course of the eighteenth century and subsequently spread right across Europe in the nineteenth. Another development was the enlargement of farms, together with the production of cereal crops, and involved taking in more marginal land for growing.

The name of Thomas Coke, 1st Earl of Leicester (1754–1842), is associated with the advances in British agriculture. Coke was a politician and lived at Holkham Hall. He took a major interest in his park and gardens, planting extensive areas of woodland. He employed Humphrey Repton to modify the design of the grounds and gardens. Coke also extended his estate, which incorporated fifty-four farms situated around the periphery.

Coke developed many innovative ideas and experimented with a range of new farming methods. He improved grasses and experimented with selective breeding methods for sheep and cattle. The resulting improvements to fodder crops served further to improve numbers and quality of sheep and cattle. He purchased strips of land and enclosed the areas; following the process that had begun in the sixteenth century. By the mid-eighteenth century there were few remaining areas of strip agriculture.

Norfolk contained distinct farming regions, which developed independently due to both different soil conditions and to local tenurial arrangements. In the central north were open fields and enclosures. In the north-west were more open fields, which supported sheep and cereal growing. The loams of Flegg in the east provided well-drained fertile arable land with open fields, and cattle grazed the marshes inland from Great Yarmouth. Open fields in the southern Breckland heathland were suited to sheep and barley. The Fenland provided pasture for sheep and cattle. The western area benefitted from improved drainage in the eighteenth and nineteenth century.

Alongside the improvements being made to agriculture, the early nineteenth century once again experienced major discontent among agricultural workers. The Corn Laws, between 1815 and 1846 kept grain prices high and

led to riots by agricultural labourers in west Norfolk. There was also an outbreak of destroying farm machinery, which was seen as threatening employment of those already on the poverty line. In 1830 there was a major episode of riots and arson across parts of the county.

COUNTRY HOUSES, ESTATES AND THE ARTS

During the Hanoverian period there was further growth in the creation of large estates, through which the landed gentry now dominated the rural countryside. The wealth that had been generated over centuries of farming can be seen expressed in their magnificent houses, set within their own private and individually designed landscapes. But these were more than just mansions set within parkland. They were working estates which were populated by their own workforces; able to deliver all their own trade and craft needs and produce their own food. These estates thus became essentially self-sufficient in all ways. Furthermore, they went on to play an integral role in the wider local economy by linking farms, villages, markets and supplying the needs of the surrounding countryside.

The principal family seats in Norfolk built in the first half of the eighteenth century included those at Felbrigg, Holkham, Houghton, Narford and Wolterton. The landscape of parklands was not an even one across the county. The larger estates were concentrated in the central north and towards the Norfolk–Suffolk border. There were fewer towards the Fens and only smaller landowners in that area. There were fewer too across the central boulder clay region, where there were historically more complex patterns of land ownership combined with higher land values. More estates were created further east but these were smaller in scale.

As well as being an outstanding politician, Sir Robert Walpole amassed a considerable fortune during his political career. He developed an understanding of architecture, pictures, sculpture, furniture and landscape design, all of which were reflected in the sumptuous surroundings of Houghton Hall, built on the site of an earlier family house. Constructed and completely furnished during the period between 1722 and 1735, Houghton Hall became a show-case for Walpole's internationally important collection of works by the finest architects, craftsmen and painters of that elegant age. The surrounding grounds and parkland were designed by Charles Bridgeman.

The famous landscape designer Humphrey Repton (1752–1818) attended Norwich Grammar School. He was apprenticed to a textile merchant in Norwich before moving to Sustead, near Aylsham, where he became sec-retary to William Windham at Felbrigg Hall and began to study botany and gardening. He became a landscape gardener, succeeding Capability Brown as the greatest landscape designer of the eighteenth century. His first commission was Catton Park, Norwich, in 1788 and his favourite project was to be Sheringham Park.

Holkham Hall is situated close to Wells-next-the-Sea. It is one of the finest examples of Palladian-style architecture and its design shows strong influences from classical Roman architecture. The house was built for Thomas Coke by the architect William Kent (1685–1748), who is recognised as having introduced the Palladian style into England.

NORFOLK AND THE GRAND TOUR

It was from the seventeenth century that aristocratic Englishmen started to venture abroad for the purposes of travel, adventure, military experience and appreciation of the arts. The example of the Paston family at Oxnead Hall was considered in the previous chapter. The term 'Grand

Tour' was developed, as this form of experience became an established way for young men to develop their education, engaging with a study of the Classics and visiting, in particular, France and Italy.

The eighteenth century saw the creation of some of Britain's most important collections. Although by no means exclusive to Norfolk, the Grand Tour underlay the formation of some of Britain's great art collections, including those at the Norfolk houses of Felbrigg, Holkham, Narford, Wolterton and Houghton. Some of Norfolk's early travellers included Ashe Windham of Felbrigg (1672–1749), Sir Andrew Fountaine of Narford (1676–1753), Thomas Coke of Holkham (1754–1842) and Horace Walpole of Houghton (1717–97). Acquisitions reflected tastes of the day and, for example, in the earlier eighteenth century works by great masters including Canaletto, Claude and Poussin were acquired to adorn the great houses of Holkham, Melton Constable, Narford and Wolterton.

It is recorded that Rev. William Gunn (1750–1841), rector of Sloley church, made the Grand Tour on two occasions. While in Rome, he discovered an important tenth-century manuscript of the *Historia Brittonum*, which he subsequently brought home and had printed to make it more widely accessible in Britain.

TRADE AND INDUSTRY

Norfolk was geographically well positioned in relation to England's increasing focus on commerce and industry, geared to the Industrial Revolution. Although it did not have the factories of the north, it did play a role in trade through the import, export and distribution of goods, including the vitally important mineral – coal.

Textile production was still the most important economic activity in Norfolk. By the mid-eighteenth century, the high point of the industry, in Norwich it employed almost half of the city's workforce. It was then to undergo a decline towards the end of eighteenth century, during a period of wider economic decline in the city.

Norfolk's geology, with its natural chalk and lime, provided the resources to facilitate glassmaking. This long historical tradition reached its peak from the seventeenth century onwards. The main focuses of glassmaking were the major seaports of Great Yarmouth and King's Lynn. A prominent producer of decorated glassware was the acclaimed William Absolom Jnr (1751–1815) of Great Yarmouth.

Brewing beer developed as an industry at many places during the eighteenth century. By 1852 there would be eighty-eight common breweries operating across Norfolk. A number of major breweries had become established by the mid-eighteenth century, mainly growing up in Norwich, Great Yarmouth and King's Lynn, with Lacon's of Yarmouth regionally prominent.

TRANSPORT

By the mid-seventeenth century a stagecoach network had been established across the country, employing four-wheeled, horse-drawn vehicles for transporting people to scheduled destinations. The condition of the roads themselves became an essential element of improving the transport infrastructure. The Turnpike Acts were introduced from the late seventeenth century whereby toll gates were set up on roads and the revenue collected was used for their upkeep. From 1769 a series of Acts were passed, enabling improvements in Norfolk's most important roads.

These were very largely those radiating out from Norwich, King's Lynn, Great Yarmouth and Fakenham in the north.

Canals were becoming a major method of transporting heavy goods in the north of England during the eighteenth century. Norfolk already had an established system of waterborne trade to which it added a canal between Norwich and Lowestoft in 1833. Bolder plans to link the east and west between King's Lynn and Norwich by canals never materialised.

SEASIDE RESORTS

It was as early as the eighteenth century that Norfolk's coast started to become a desirable destination for visitors. Fashionable members of society started to look to the Norfolk coast in search of leisure pursuits and sea bathing. The sandy beaches of Great Yarmouth provided an obvious attraction and became the first major draw. A bathing machine was constructed there in 1779 and a bath house was located on the beach in 1814.

The fishing village of Cromer developed into another popular seaside location, attracting visitors from the end of the eighteenth century. This resort was to became popular among the more affluent families, who built not only seaside houses there, but also permanent homes in the vicinity.

NORFOLK AND THE WIDER WORLD

Norfolk's Regiment, still known as the 9th Foot, was involved in campaigns across the world between 1714 and 1837, ranging from the Americas to Asia. In 1761 the Regiment fought the French at Belle Isle in the Bay of Biscay and served in Cuba in the following year. Subsequent years saw a series of major international conflicts. In 1776 they were sent to Quebec and took part in the war against the American colonies in Canada and North America. They were part of the army of General Burgoyne, which surrendered at Saratoga in 1777. Following a return to Britain, the 9th was stationed in the West Indies in 1788.

At the end of the eighteenth century it was given the distinction of bearing Britannia as the Regimental badge. The American War of Independence was followed by the Napoleonic Wars and the 9th went on to serve with distinction throughout the Peninsular War, between 1808 and 1814. The Regiment was always seen in the forefront of battles and won nine additional battle honours in the campaign. In 1835 it was sent to India for the first time, which was to be the start of a longstanding association with that country, lasting for over a century.

During the period of the Napoleonic Wars coastal defences were constructed against possible foreign hostility. In fact, there had been the potential of seaborne invasion for much of the eighteenth century. Whilst Britain was at war with America, there was a threat from not only France but also Spain and Holland. There were already forts at Great Yarmouth and at King's Lynn, St Anne's fort was re-armed. A battery was placed at Cromer and another five were positioned at Great Yarmouth. These all remained active when war with France began in 1793. In 1803 an additional battery was placed at Weybourne. This was followed by others across north Norfolk. These defences were maintained until Napoleon's defeat in 1815.

This period saw some of Norfolk's most famous citizens make contributions to the establishment of the modern world. Thomas Paine (1737–1809) was born in White Hart Street, Thetford, son of a local farmer. This extraordinary man managed to change the world through his influence on international affairs on a major scale. He was an author, pamphleteer, inventor, intellectual and revolutionary. He was one of the Founding Fathers of the United States and participated in the American Revolution. Through his writings, which were powerful expressions of man's rights, he stimulated people worldwide. At the height of his fame, his books were read in their hundreds of thousands. After returning to England he needed to flee to France to escape prosecution for his writing. There, he was to greatly influence the French Revolution. He also actively contributed to the Industrial Revolution, as a designer of the cast-iron bridge. His book, *The Rights of Man* (1791), served as a guide to ideas of 'enlightenment' at this turbulent time in world history. Paine died in Greenwich Village, New York City, at the age of 72. His ideas have continued to resonate down the generations.

Norfolk's most famous son, Horatio Nelson, was born slightly later than Paine, in Burnham Thorpe, north Norfolk, in 1758. He enjoyed an outstanding career as a naval commander and his exploits made him a national hero. He is renowned for his inspirational leadership and bold, decisive actions. Nelson distinguished himself in the defeat of the Spanish off Cape Vincent in 1797, which was followed by his victory at the Battle of the Nile. It was at the Battle of Copenhagen in 1801 that, when given the order to retreat in the face of fierce bombardment from shore batteries, he famously raised his telescope to his blind eye and declared that he could see no signal to withdraw. He went on to achieve another famous victory. In 1803 he was made Commander-in-Chief of the Mediterranean fleet and given HMS *Victory* as his flagship.

Between 1794 and 1805, the Royal Navy maintained a vital supremacy over the French. Nelson's final victory was the Battle of Trafalgar (1805). Despite being fatally wounded, he had saved Britain from the threat of invasion by Napoleon. He was awarded a state funeral, which was held at St Paul's Cathedral in London in 1806. Although Nelson is famously reported as saying 'I am a Norfolk man and glory in being so', his career ultimately led him away from the county of his birth. He continued to visit Great Yarmouth, which was an important naval depot and garrison town. His close association with Norfolk was memorialised with the erection of a monumental column to him in Great Yarmouth in 1817.

CRIME AND PUNISHMENT

There was no standing police force in Georgian England. When crimes were detected, punishments were severe and the death penalty was enforced for what we would today consider to be relatively minor issues. However, some more serious offences needed to be confronted.

It was in the eighteenth century that smuggling became a serious problem on a national scale. It was a particularly well-organised practice around Norfolk's seaboard, where local gangs defied the authorities. The underlying cause for the escalation in smuggling had been the level of taxation imposed on imported goods to pay for the increasingly expensive wars of the period. It fell to the army to confront what were in effect private militias across the county's villages and beaches, particularly in the area between Snettisham and Wells. It was not until Prime Minister William Pitt lowered customs duties in the 1780s that the activities of the smugglers were rendered unprofitable and the practice was effectively curtailed.

The practice of highway robbery was similarly prevalent. One particularly notorious highwayman plied his illegal trade in Norfolk and adjacent counties. In 1737 a horse dealer named John Palmer took up residence at Long Sutton, in the Lincolnshire fens. His real and more famous name was Dick Turpin (1705–39) and he robbed stagecoaches on roads between Norfolk and London. When Turpin's true identity was eventually discovered, he was captured and hanged in York in 1739.

As the fear of crime maintained its grip through the eighteenth century, so punishments handed down by the judicial system became ever more harsh. The most common form of punishment at this time was execution by public hanging. Public executions of convicted prisoners were carried out at the foot of the stone bridge at Norwich Castle, where these gruesome events attracted large crowds.

Prison conditions were similarly horrific, exacerbated by overcrowding. Elizabeth Fry (1780–1845) was a Quaker and social reformer, born in Norwich to the Gurney banking family. Influenced by visits to Newgate Prison in London, she became a prison reformer. She campaigned for the provision of schooling for children imprisoned with their mothers and for the improved conditions of prisoners. She also campaigned for the rights of prisoners sentenced to transportation. Elizabeth later created a training school for nurses, which in turn was an influence on Florence Nightingale.

The exploration of the wider world provided new opportunities for dealing with criminals, many of whom had been convicted of relatively minor offences. New territories were being explored and a new land was discovered, which was called 'New Holland', and which is known to us today as Australia. Transportation was introduced as a new form of punishment in 1714 and criminals were sent away to a new prison colony at Botany Bay, called Sydney.

It was at Norwich Castle that prisoners were held prior to their transportation. Ties have been established over many years between the city and the descendants of early transportees who had been held in Norwich Castle gaol. The stories of many families are well recorded. Mary Ann Adams from Norfolk was convicted of stealing a purse and sent to Sydney, where she married another transportee named Thomas Richardson, in 1837.

One of the most famous transportees was Henry Kable (1763–1846), who had been convicted of a burglary at Thetford in 1783. When in Norwich gaol, Henry met Susannah Holmes and they managed to conceive a son while in prison. When they eventually reached Botany Bay in 1788, Henry and Susannah married. Together, they raised eleven children. In 1988, 500 of their descendants came together to celebrate Henry and Susannah's 200th wedding anniversary. The couple are recognised as one of Australia's founding families and their descendants still regularly visit Norwich Castle.

THE ARTS

The label of 'restless age' may also be applied to this period through the arts, in terms of influences from abroad and foreign travel. Through the agencies of warfare and thirst for knowledge and enlightenment, Norfolk's citizens brought back exotic items from Europe, America, Australia, Asia, Africa and the Pacific. There was an increasing desire to explore and record other world cultures, resulting in the creation of provocative new art and literature.

In the field of literature and progressive thinking, Thomas Paine has already been mentioned. Another writer, Amelia Opie (1769–1853), who was born and lived in Norwich, was an author of novels and poetry. Through such novels as *Adeline Mowbray* (1804) she explored serious issues of the day including the position of women in society and that of slavery. Following the death of her husband in 1807, she stopped writing fiction and focused her attention on charitable work, helping in prisons, workhouses and hospitals. She also became known as a leading abolitionist. Amelia bought a house in Norwich adjacent to Castle Meadow and the location is now called Opie Street.

The work of the finest architects enhanced the great country houses, such as Houghton Hall and Holkham Hall. Great art collections were being formed by Sir Robert Walpole and other wealthy individuals. Landscape design has also left a major mark on the Norfolk countryside.

In painting, the Norwich Society of Artists was founded in 1803 by John Crome (1768–1821) and his friend Robert Ladbrooke. It brought together professional painters, drawing masters and amateurs, becoming what was then the only regional school of painting in England. John Sell Cotman (1782–1842) joined the Society in 1807 and became one of its great masters. Other members of what became known as 'The Norwich School' were John Berney Crome, George Vincent, James Stark, Joseph and Alfred Stannard, John Thirtle, Thomas Lound and Henry Ninham. This association of artists found their inspiration in the heaths and woodland of East Anglia, together with rivers, such as the Yare, and the Norfolk coast. They flourished as a group throughout the first half of the nineteenth century.

The work of the Norwich School of

painters was based on realism, derived from direct obser-
vation of the local landscape. It represented a departure
from the tradition of classical landscape as seen in the
work of Claude and Poussin. Their influences included the
tradition of Dutch landscape painting, including such artists as Jacob van Ruisdael and Albert Cuyp. In turn, the
influence of the Norwich School paved the way for the
great British tradition of landscape painting, in particular
through the work on John Constable and J.M.W. Turner.

THE CLOSE OF THE HANOVERIAN DYNASTY

In 1837 William IV, last king of the House of Hanover,
died after a seven-year reign. England had embarked on
a period of industrial and social change, together with a
rapidly growing population and accompanied by underlying social tensions. William left no surviving legitimate
children and he was succeeded by his niece, Victoria.

While in some ways Norfolk and its citizens were engaged
in events on a wider national and international scale, by the
end of the Hanoverian period it was beginning to experience
an economic downturn. In the final years of the eighteenth
century Norwich itself no longer enjoyed its earlier commercial importance. Signs of a decline might perhaps be
interpreted through the eyes of the Norwich School artists,
much of whose work may perhaps be viewed as reflecting
the county in idyllic terms, with a nostalgic eye; encapsulat-
ing a time of Norfolk's former greatness.

9

THE VICTORIANS TO THE GREAT WAR

1837–1914

Queen Victoria was crowned monarch in 1837, following the death of her uncle William IV (r. 1830–37). The Victorian age bore witness to events that shaped our modern world. It was a period of relative peace between the great international powers. Great Britain established a major global presence and there was significantly increased economic activity. The population of England and Wales more than doubled between the mid-nineteenth century and the beginning of the twentieth century, from seventeen million to forty million.

In the mid-nineteenth century there were 443,000 people living in Norfolk. The county was not industrialised to the extent seen in other parts of Britain. Here, most people were still living off of the land. In the early decades, everyday life for rural people remained much as it had been in previous centuries. Families lived in cottages without access to running water, sewerage, public education, healthcare or efficient methods of transport. As the century progressed, the Victorian years gave rise to steady improvements in living conditions, alongside other progressive changes in public health, social provision, commerce and across the arts.

The middle years of the nineteenth century saw the introduction of liberal legislation through a series of new laws. In 1838 the Abolition of Slavery Act came into force. A poor law was introduced to provide relief for the destitute. In 1870 the Education Act was passed, which introduced universal education. The Chartist movement between 1836 and 1848 sought political rights for the working classes. The period also witnessed the last public execution, in 1868.

From the 1840s the railways became the principal conduit for trade. Norfolk's major towns achieved improved connections with other parts of the country and, in particular, London.

VICTORIAN VALUES

The period from the 1780s to the 1840s had been one of increasing disorder. In Victorian England, strong efforts were made to reduce lawlessness, drunkenness, general crime and domestic violence, and to subdue political unrest. In order to achieve this, it was considered a priority to address the issue of moral values and behaviour, while promoting Christian morality. The approach employed was the creation of a set of values embodying the 'Spirit of the Age', involving adhesion to religion, domesticity and stability of home life, a strong work ethic and desire for personal improvement.

These efforts involved all sectors of society, including churches, schools, the newly established police force and many voluntary bodies, as well as parliament and the courts. By the 1870s a noticeable decline in crime, drunkenness and unsociable behaviour had been achieved.

Punishments for crimes remained severe and hangings were a regular public spectacle until 1868. In Norfolk, executions were performed outside Norwich Castle and the author Charles Dickens described visiting Norwich to see one such hanging.

Victorian society was strongly religious, with over 40 per cent of the population regularly going to church, and with more than half of those people attending Nonconformist chapels. The proportion of churchgoers in Norfolk was higher than in other parts of the country. The church was to become a cornerstone of the community and part of the routine of family life, with attendance considered the norm. As more people moved to the towns, new churches were built in the developing areas and many older ones were restored.

SCHOOLS

The basic form of educational provision for the poor in Victorian England was the Dame School. These establishments varied in quality. While some just provided a form of day care, others managed to deliver a sound, if basic, education. Significant improvement was made during the late nineteenth century, following the Education Act of 1870. By the final decades of the century there was adequate provision of school places for all children.

During the second half of the century a broader access to education was assisted by the provision of classes for adults and the establishment of lending libraries. Some villages also provided reading rooms. Sunday schools, which had been established in the late eighteenth century, were also widely available. By the 1850s, the level of literacy was increasing significantly.

THE ARRIVAL OF THE RAILWAYS

The first Norfolk railway was opened in 1844 and ran between Norwich and Great Yarmouth. A connection from Norwich to London was made the following year. By 1850 all major towns across Norfolk had been joined by rail. The different lines came together under the Eastern Counties Railway in 1854 and subsequently became the Great Eastern Railway in 1862.

Norfolk's rail network was widespread and intricate, essentially linking the market towns and coastal resorts. The establishment of the system had a positive influence on the commercial stability and subsequent development of the county, especially Norwich. The railways also provided a welcome source of employment, particularly through the Great Eastern Railway.

THE TOWNS

England in the eighteenth and nineteenth centuries was becoming the first truly urban nation. In Norfolk, conditions in the countryside increasingly drove a migration to the towns during Victoria's reign, leading to a need for a massive increase in urban housing.

At the start of the Victorian era, Norwich was experiencing an economic decline and a series of social problems. The city had lost its prominence in the textile industry, together with its status as England's second city. The citizens had started to protest about low wages, high food prices and unemployment, exacerbated by the introduction of power looms. Industrial pollution from factories, power stations and the railway, together with cramped housing conditions, combined to make the city a dirty and often unpleasant place. In spite of these problems, it nearly doubled in size, from 62,000 inhabitants to 112,000, between 1837 and the end of Victoria's reign in 1901.

For the next sixty years, steady improvements were made to address the accumulated problems. Better communications with other parts of the country, the new forms of transport and a growth of new industries served to re-establish Norwich as a fine city as it approached the twentieth century. There were civic improvements, including the building of terraced houses, with episodes of rapid construction in the north and north-eastern suburbs. Important new buildings were built, involving some prominent architects. Edward Boardman (1833–1910) designed the Norfolk and Norwich Hospital and undertook the conversion of the historic Norwich Castle into a museum. George Skipper (1846–1948) designed the Royal Arcade, with its stunning Art Nouveau entrance. Skipper also created the acclaimed palazzo of the Norwich Union office building. Norwich's second cathedral, the Cathedral Church of St John the Baptist, was designed by George Gilbert Scott Jr and constructed between 1882 and 1910.

By the 1890s, Norwich had three railway stations and trams were introduced in 1900. A sewer system was constructed in 1869. Public parks were created at Chapelfield and on Mousehold Heath, where there was an ornate bandstand. By the end of the Victorian period, Norwich had become a peaceful, law-abiding and prosperous city once again.

George Skipper also left his architectural mark on the profile of Cromer, which was developing as a seaside resort. He designed some nineteen distinctive new buildings there, including the Hotel de Paris, which remains as a striking feature of today's skyline.

Norfolk's second town was still Great Yarmouth, with a population of 28,000 in 1837. Its importance was based on maritime trade, dealing in Baltic timber, cargoes from the Rhineland and exporting corn from East Anglia. But it was herrings, known as 'silver darlings', that created the greatest wealth and new markets for them were opened up with the railways. Yarmouth was England's eighth most important port and fishing centre until the end of the nineteenth century. The fishing fleet was supplemented each autumn by the arrival of Scottish vessels. Together, they maintained a trade in salted herring with eastern Europe. Yarmouth's herring fishery continued to grow in importance and its greatest season was in 1913, when the fleet numbered over 1,000 steam and sailing drifters, landing 900 million fish. Every autumn there was also an influx of hundreds of Scottish fisherwomen who came to gut, salt and pack the herring. The town resonated to the sounds of the fish wharves and the smell of the smokehouses, where kippers were hung on wooden staves called 'spits'.

The growing holiday industry was given a boost by the arrival of the railway. Like Norwich, Great Yarmouth had three stations by the end of the century. Holidaymakers arrived from London by train and also by paddle steamer from the Thames Estuary. Others came from the Midlands, direct to the Beach Station. The Wellington Pier was constructed in 1853, followed by the Britannia Pier in 1858. The Marine Parade was extended and developed in 1863.

Gorleston to the south, with its wide sandy beaches, developed as a quieter family resort.

King's Lynn retained its importance as a trading port. It maintained a coastal trade in grain and coal, as well as fishing. It was also an important market town, serving west Norfolk and the eastern Fens. In 1867–69 the Alexandra Dock was built, followed by the Bentinck Dock in 1883. Both enabled larger ships to access the port, while the railway was extended to the wharves. Living conditions had improved markedly by the end of the nineteenth century. Following a typhoid epidemic in 1897, clean water was provided for the town through a new waterworks. The population grew from 16,000 in 1837 to 24,000 at the end of the century.

INDUSTRIAL NORFOLK

The Industrial Revolution eventually made a belated appearance in Norfolk. Food processing became an important industry, most famously through Colman's of Norwich. Jeremiah Colman founded the company in 1814 and it steadily expanded to become a regional institution. The distinctive yellow branding famous today was introduced in 1855 and in 1866 Colman's were given a Royal Warrant as manufacturers of mustard to Queen Victoria; one which continues to the present day. Besides being a major employer, the Colmans were pioneers in social welfare, devoted to the health and welfare of their workers. They employed the first ever industrial nurse in Britain, Philippa Flowerday, and also a works doctor, as well as running a Sick Benefit Society and establishing a school for the children of workers.

Norwich also became a centre for engineering, particularly through Barnard, Bishop and Barnards, who set up their ironworks at Coslany in 1851, and Boulton and Paul, at Mountergate, in 1865–91. By 1870 leatherworking had become Norwich's leading industry, with an emphasis on shoe manufacture. It was boot and shoe making that replaced textiles as the major employer in Norwich.

In the financial sector, Norwich was a centre for banking and insurance. The local Gurney Bank became part of Barclays in 1896. In the sphere of life insurance, Norwich Union Fire and Life Societies became established nationally.

The late eighteenth and nineteenth centuries saw further growth of beer making, with Norfolk's breweries supplying establishments between Lincolnshire and Essex. A.J. Caley & Son started as chemists and went on to produce cocoa and chocolate. Norwich also remained a major agricultural centre, with a thriving cattle market in the centre of the city, adjacent to the castle. Associated trades grew up in adjacent streets, with butchers in and around Ber Street.

One of the more unusual trades carried out in Norwich was brush making. Brushes had been made in the city from the eighteenth century and by 1890 there were fifteen manufacturers in the city, including S.D. Page & Sons, the largest in the country. This also became a major established trade at Wymondham.

During the later nineteenth and twentieth centuries one of the most popular family leisure activities was going to fairgrounds, which travelled all over the country. All ages would be captivated by the colourful, noisy and exotic amusement rides. The most famous and popular attraction was the carousel, or merry-go-round. Savages of King's Lynn is the name associated with the construction of these extravagant rides. Its engines and machinery were once familiar all over Britain and abroad. The name remains firmly linked with King's Lynn, where the company was a major employer. Established by Frederick Savage in 1853, his firm first produced horse-drawn agricultural machinery and then self-propelled traction engines, eventually developing showground machinery in 1872.

There were numerous small iron foundries during the early nineteenth century. Some of these grew to become larger engineering works. It was in the mid-nineteenth century that Thetford became the centre of a heavy engineering industry. Charles Burrell & Sons were manufacturers of some of the most highly regarded steam locomotives in the world through the nineteenth and early twentieth centuries. They built steam traction engines, agricultural machinery, steam trucks and steam engines. At the height of their business the firm employed over 350 people in the town. Members of the Burrell family had grown their business from origins in metal smithing in the 1740s. During the later years of the eighteenth century, Joseph Burrell began to develop and manufacture agricultural implements and early in the nineteenth century he began to design patent agricultural machinery with his brothers, James and William. During the mid-nineteenth century they developed a self-propelled road engine for pulling loads, known as the Burrell-Boydell engine.

THE LAND

Although Norfolk was situated well away from the coalfields and the major centres of heavy industry that proliferated to the west and north, the county played a significant role in support of the Industrial Revolution through what can be called the Agricultural Revolution. The country's population grew rapidly over these years and Norfolk's agriculture made a significant contribution to feeding them.

Agriculture was still the county's main employer and was to remain so until the beginning of the twentieth century.

Landholdings of the landed gentry with their grand houses, lakes, parks, farms and associated villages still dominated large parts of the county during the later nineteenth century, particularly in the north. Some of the great estates had increased in size during the later eighteenth century and by the middle years of the nineteenth century, more than 100 Norfolk families owned estates greater than 2,000 acres. Their distinctive landscapes were designed to accommodate field sports, as well as the husbandry of game herds. Holkham remained the largest, while others of the period included Houghton Hall, the Raynham Estate, Melton Constable and Wolterton.

The construction of grand houses continued in the Victorian years, although the styles employed and the scale differed from their heyday in the previous century. New builds included Costessey Hall near Norwich (1826–55), built as an extension to a Tudor house, Cromer Hall (1856–60), Bylaugh Hall (1849–51), Lynford Hall (1856–61), in addition to How Hill House, Kelling Hall, South Pickenham Hall and Sandringham House.

It was in the 1860s that Edward, Prince of Wales, later to become King Edward VII, acquired Sandringham, situated just to the north of King's Lynn, as his private residence and estate. The main house was built in 1870 to accommodate the royal family and has remained in their hands ever since. An agricul-

tural recession that started in the 1870s eventually brought an end to the construction of more grand country houses.

The years between 1840 and 1870 had seen agriculture in Norfolk flourish, with the development of what is known as 'High Farming'. The term denoted 'top quality' farming, associated with the adoption of new methods to achieve improved results. The practices in question were improvements in land drainage, use of fertilisers, intensive livestock production and new designs in farm buildings to achieve animal fattening and greater efficiency. The adoption of machinery steadily increased, in particular the use of steam engines produced by Burrells in Thetford.

Things then changed dramatically during the mid-1870s. There was a collapse in grain prices and an accompanying agricultural depression right across the country. Landowners suffered a significant decline in income from rents. Living conditions for rural communities was already poor and although some estates did provide limited housing for labourers, hovels were more common. The threat of starvation encouraged ever greater numbers of farmworkers to migrate to the towns.

It was not until after 1894 that the countryside experienced a slow but steady recovery. The years leading up to 1914 then saw good quality produce finding markets, especially through malting, barley, livestock and dairying. In the Fenland, the growing of fruit and vegetables continued to thrive.

The life of Sir George Edwards (1850–1933) serves to illustrate many aspects of country life and the importance of agriculture within the county. Born at Marsham, near Aylsham, George was the youngest of seven children from a poor family. At the age of just 5, he entered the local workhouse with his family. When they came out, George immediately started work on the land, given the job of scaring crows.

At the age of 17, he became an agricultural worker and was employed as a ploughman. At 22 he married Charlotte Corke, who taught him to read and write, and he proceeded to become a Methodist lay preacher. In the 1870s George became secretary of the local branch of the Agricultural Labourer's Union. He entered local politics as a Liberal, pressing for land reform and the vote for farmworkers. His lasting achievement was the foundation of the Eastern Counties Agricultural Union in 1906, which was to become the National Union of Agricultural Workers after the Great War.

In 1920, at the age of 70, George Edwards was elected to Parliament as Labour candidate for South Norfolk. He was awarded the OBE in 1929 and in 1933, the year he died, became the first farmworker to be knighted. This remarkable man had overcome poverty, illiteracy and low birth, devoting his whole life to the service of his fellow man.

The Victorian years overall witnessed a decline in rural populations. From the 1850s onwards, an unforeseen impact of the railway was to further facilitate the migration of people away from Norfolk to London and to the north of England. Others were lured further afield by opportunities offered in Canada and America.

WORKHOUSES

Workhouse buildings are still found across Norfolk and serve as a reminder of rural poverty during the nineteenth century. There had been a steady increase in unemployment since the end of the Napoleonic Wars in 1815. In the countryside, this was exacerbated by the impact of new technology at the expense of jobs for agricultural workers. The New Poor Law of 1834 sought to address the relief of poverty in society.

Although workhouses, which had been introduced in the eighteenth century, were able to provide relief for the truly destitute, the conditions provided for inmates were such that they would deter all but the really needy.

The new Act resulted in the formation of new 'unions' between adjacent parishes. These ensured better provision of workhouse accommodation for the poor. The formation of the unions enabled the joint financing of workhouse provision across all areas.

Between 1835 and 1838, twelve unions were formed in Norfolk and built new workhouses while, in other areas, existing buildings continued to be used. Inmates lived and worked under a strict regime in return for their accommodation and food. The workhouse at Gressenhall near East Dereham in central Norfolk has been preserved as a museum, where the lives of the inmates can be explored. Originally built in 1777, from 1834 Gressenhall became the workhouse for the Mitford and Launditch area.

WINDPUMPS AND WINDMILLS

During the later eighteenth and nineteenth centuries, the sight of drainage windmills or windpumps dominated large parts of Norfolk's flatter landscape. These buildings were constructed primarily in the east to remove excess water from the surface of marshy areas. The most famous example of a windpump is that at St Benet's Abbey, which was constructed inside a medieval abbey gatehouse during the later eighteenth century and has been a subject for many artists.

The landscape of Broadland provides the densest landscape of these mills anywhere in England. The very early examples were constructed from timber but most surviving mills are brick towers, which still dominate the flat marshy landscape inland from Great Yarmouth.

The early ones were manually turned while later examples employed a fantail mechanism. Steam engines were also used from the mid-nineteenth century.

Norfolk's landscape also favoured the establishment and use of windmills for producing corn. Over 400 corn mills were in use in the county around 1850. By the outbreak of the First World War in 1914, this had declined to just 100.

TRANSPORT AND TRADE

The improvements in transport allowed quicker journeys across the country, enabling daily deliveries over long distances and providing a boost to the economy. Additions to the early railway system provided improvements to the lines serving the coastal tourist resorts. Tramways were also established between the rail lines and docks at King's Lynn, Great Yarmouth and Wells, facilitating the loading of commercial commodities to rail wagons.

As in medieval times, waterways continued to be of importance for transporting heavy goods. Rivers to the west of the central Norfolk watershed were linked with King's Lynn and the Fenland. Those to the east were linked to Great Yarmouth. In 1872 the North Walsham and Dilham canal connected Dilham with Antingham to the north. Further west, the River Bure was improved and widened as far inland as Aylsham. Both of these systems had mills located on their banks.

The sight of the majestic sailing vessels called wherries, with their distinctive sails and low, rounded profile, is inextricably associated with Norfolk's Broads. Wherries are a form of sailing barge that were the main means of transporting traded goods between Norwich and Great Yarmouth. They could each carry up to 50 tons, with their cargoes of coal, grain, timber, building materials and fertilisers, which they carried along the River Yare and across Broadland. The use of wherries eventually declined during the twentieth century, although a few remained until the outbreak of the Second World War.

The seafaring importance of Norfolk's coast extended beyond the large towns. The smaller ports, including Wells, Blakeney, Cley and Burnham, were still engaged in the import of coal, timber and building materials and the export of grain. Together with other coastal villages including Sheringham and Weybourne, they had their own longshore fishing fleets. A wooden jetty still functioned at Cromer to facilitate the loading of farming produce onto sea-going vessels.

THE SEASIDE

Norfolk's seaside was becoming an increasingly fashionable attraction, while providing a lift to the county's economy in a new direction. Businessmen began to invest in bathing machines and other aspects related to tourism. The need for places for visitors to stay increased and guest houses and hotels grew up at resorts right around the coast. Grand new architectural interventions started to characterise the coastal resorts.

The earlier jetty at Cromer was replaced by a longer structure in 1846 and visitors to the resort began to use it as a promenade. Then a new pier was constructed in 1902, specifically designed for public use and enjoyment. At Great Yarmouth, Wellington Pier was opened in 1853, with the nearby Britannia Pier built just five years later. In 1903 they were accompanied by a Pavilion and a Winter Gardens. Hunstanton in the west originally received visitors as a watering place. It later became popular with visitors from the east Midlands as a seaside resort.

It was the arrival of the railway that provided the critical boost to Norfolk's seaside industry. A line connecting Great Yarmouth to Norwich opened in 1844 and subsequent lines linked to Cromer, Sheringham and Mundesley, which enabled them to grow as seaside destinations.

INTERNATIONAL INFLUENCES

The English East India Company had been founded in 1600 to pursue trade in the East Indies (South East Asia) and came to own large parts of India. In 1858 the rule of what was by then the British East India Company was handed over to the Crown. The Indian subcontinent was to remain under British rule until 1947; the period known as the British Raj. The Punjab was an independent kingdom in the north-west of India and came under British control in 1805. The Maharajah Duleep Singh (1839–93) was the last Sikh ruler of the region. Singh was to spend most of his life in England and have a lifelong association with the area around Thetford.

It was following the Anglo-Sikh wars of the 1860s that the young Duleep Singh surrendered his lands and property and was exiled to England, aged just 15. In 1863 he purchased the Elveden Estate, on the Norfolk–Suffolk border, which he transformed into an oriental palace. Outside, exotic peacocks roamed the grounds, while cheetahs and leopards were kept in enclosures. As the years passed, Singh adopted the life of an English gentleman and became renowned as a colourful local personality. He was befriended by Queen Victoria, who was godmother to several of his eight children. He is buried in Elveden churchyard.

During the nineteenth century, a number of European tourists visited Egypt. Many brought back artefacts and formed their own collections. Some Norfolk residents played high-profile roles in the European discovery of ancient Egypt. One of these was Howard Carter (1873–1939), of Swaffham, who discovered the tomb of Tutankhamun, which was one of the most famous and spectacular archaeological discoveries ever made. Sir Henry Rider Haggard (1856–1925), the famous writer, was also born and lived in Norfolk. A keen traveller, he too was fascinated by Egypt. He bought antiquities and donated some items to the Norwich Museum in 1917.

Rider Haggard's writings reflect a contemporary fascination with the investigation of ancient and exotic cultures. He was also an accomplished farmer on his own Norfolk estate and in 1902 he published *Rural England*, a study of agriculture and rural conditions in Britain at the time. His life brings together the associations of agriculture and exploration overseas alongside the important literary tradition that has developed within the county.

International politics and the maintenance of the British Empire involved the Royal Norfolk Regiment. In 1835, they arrived in India. From there they were sent to Afghanistan and took part in bitter hand-to-hand fighting at the Khyber Pass. They participated in the First Sikh War of 1845. When in 1854 England declared war on Russia, they were sent to the Crimean War.

In 1857 the 9th Foot became a two-battalion regiment. Towards the end of the nineteenth century both battalions were involved in campaigns to stabilise the security of the British Empire. They served in the Second Afghan War, Gibraltar, India and Burma. On 1 July 1881 they became The Norfolk Regiment. In 1900 they were sent to South Africa to participate in the Boer War.

SPORT IN VICTORIAN NORFOLK

The formal organisation of major sports at this time played an integral role in the efforts to define and promote Victorian moral values. Organised sport was a significant cultural invention of Victorian England and became a way of focusing the energies and behaviour of all social classes. Sports such as cricket, rugby union and football all encouraged the kind of virtues and values seen as important to ensure a stable, considerate and fair society. Sports clubs were established throughout the county.

Cricket had been played in Norfolk from the seventeenth century. It was in 1876 that Norfolk County Cricket Club was founded. The Eastern Counties Rugby Union, which organised the game across Norfolk, Suffolk and Essex, was founded in 1890. The Norfolk and Suffolk Football League was established in 1897, bringing together the clubs Beccles Claxton, Great Yarmouth Town, Kirkley, Lowestoft Town, Lynn Town and Norwich CEYMS. Both Norwich City and Ipswich Town joined in the years after 1900. Norwich City FC was founded in 1902.

THE ARTS

The tradition of writing in Norfolk blossomed in the Victorian period. Sir Henry Rider Haggard's novels include *King Solomon's Mines* and *She*. Anna Sewell (1820–78) was born in Great Yarmouth. She wrote her only but internationally acclaimed novel *Black Beauty* at her house at Old Catton, on the outskirts of Norwich. Charles Dickens (1812–70) visited Norfolk on occasions and in his novel *David Copperfield*, he included an evocative description of Great Yarmouth in 1850.

In the field of photography, Norfolk's Olive Edis (1876–1955) rose to international renown through her portrait photography and as a war artist during the First World War. She opened a studio at Sheringham, on the north coast, in 1903, from where she specialised in portraits of fishermen and local gentry.

Edis pioneered new photographic techniques through the early decades of the twentieth century. She photographed a wide variety of British society, from royalty and famous people to studies of Norfolk fishermen and their families. Her more prominent sitters included George Bernard Shaw, Thomas Hardy, Emmeline Pankhurst and the Duke of York.

When the First World War started, Edis was appointed an official war artist and became the only official woman photographer. During the course of this work, she photographed the various women's services and the battlefields of France and Flanders between 1914 and 1918.

Peter Henry Emerson (1856–1936) was another photographer and writer, who was best known for his evocative images of rural life in Norfolk and Suffolk. He liked to depict real people in their own environment and he used his photography to capture and preserve what he recognised as disappearing ways of life.

In an age of rapidly expanding industrialisation and styles, Thomas Jeckyll (1827–81) became an influential figure in the Victorian design reform movement. He was also a major designer of private and public architecture. Jeckyll's architectural career was focused on East Anglia. Today, he is perhaps best known for his metalwork designs, which combined oriental influences and include some of the finest pieces of the period. He established his name designing exhibition pieces for the Norwich ironwork firm of Barnard, Bishop and Barnards, with whom he won international awards for such pieces as the Norwich Gates, shown at the 1862 London International Exhibition, and which are now installed at Sandringham.

Norwich's Castle Museum has its origins in Victorian Norfolk. The Norfolk and Norwich Museum was established in 1825, initially located in the city's Haymarket. By the 1880s it had become apparent that Norwich Castle was no longer adequate to serve as a gaol and it was replaced by a new county prison that was constructed on Mousehold Heath, to the north of the city. It was local architect Edward Boardman, together with local banker John Gurney (1819–90), who recognised the potential for redeveloping the castle to house the museum. Norwich Corporation purchased the site in 1884 and Boardman himself prepared the plans for the new museum, based on the conversion of the Norman Keep and prison buildings. Boardman's proposal to reinsert the lost Norman principal floor and replicate the original Norman castle interior was rejected by the museum committee on cost grounds – a plan that is at last being revived and realised in 2020.

THE FINAL YEARS

Queen Victoria died in 1901. By the time of her death, her reign had seen major improvements in living conditions across Norfolk. These included the introduction of water mains, sewers, paved streets, gas lighting, surfaced roads, organised sport and even newspapers, which in turn enabled the swift communication of national news and events. Houses were now routinely built in brick or stone. There were further improvements in education and provision for the poor and destitute. New methods of transport opened up the county to improved trade and mass tourism. The first cars were appearing on the roads. The crisis in public order had been tackled and a strong moral code embraced.

The years following Victoria's death saw low unemployment but a rise in the cost of living. A changing political landscape began to emerge, together with a surge in Trades Union membership. But all was to be violently disrupted by international events in just the second decade of the twentieth century.

10

THE WAR YEARS

1914–45

The first half of the twentieth century was dominated by two world wars. Norfolk's location, with its proximity to Europe and Scandinavia, together with its long, exposed beaches, left it vulnerable to potential attack and invasion at every stage. Although invasion remained just a threat, its towns and their populations suffered badly from aerial and naval bombardment on both occasions. Generations of its young servicemen and women were lost in service. Both periods of national conflict and their intervening years also had a profound economic impact on the county, from which it took decades to recover.

Norfolk's rural character and location away from London and the south-east meant that it was able to make a useful contribution to the nation in both wars. Its position as a major agricultural resource was important for the survival of the whole country during times of austerity. Its unique topography and situation also made it a well-positioned military training ground as well as an ideal location for airfields, as aerial warfare became an increasingly decisive factor in determining the outcome of major conflicts during the twentieth century.

Norfolk was subjected to large invasions of service personnel, followed by rapid depopulations, which again had a destabilising impact on the regional economy and infrastructure. Its own Norfolk Regiment played important roles right across the globe during both world wars.

THE OUTBREAK OF THE FIRST WORLD WAR

The year 1914 saw the start of the first world conflict. The reasons for the outbreak are complex and remain controversial, as well as peripheral to so many of those who suffered and who lost their lives. The war was relentlessly pursued and led to a terrible cost in terms of both lives lost and economic resources, which impoverished much of Europe. Its onset led to three decades of world instability, violence and suffering on an unprecedented scale.

The First World War was to change life in Norfolk profoundly. A generation of its young men went off to fight. Approximately 100,000 of Norfolk's youth served in the armed forces, of whom over 12,000 did not return.

A wave of early enthusiasm swept the county and everything was immediately geared up for the war. Britain's army was voluntary in 1914 and young men were initially eager to join the armed forces. Some local firms, such as Colman's, offered guarantees that jobs would be held open for employees who enlisted. Once fighting started in earnest, the terrible losses sustained meant that, in 1916, conscription needed to be introduced. The process of mobilisation saw training camps established across the county.

Norfolk remained ever-alert to the threat of invasion. Pillboxes were positioned across the county. Some examples still remain, including those at North Walsham and in the vicinity of Great Yarmouth.

Britain's food supply from abroad was threatened by attacks from German U-boats on shipping. At home, all efforts were made towards maximising food production and the overall effect was to give a boost to Norfolk's agricultural capability. There was less manpower available and an appeal was made for women to replace the agricultural workers who had gone off to war. Female land workers were to become a common sight.

Other sectors of the workforce had also been depleted. Women undertook jobs of all kinds, including factory work, such as in Colman's Mustard factory and in local shoe manufacture. Norfolk's industries became geared towards the support of the military effort, producing munitions, uniforms and a range of components.

THE WAR REACHES NORFOLK

Although so much of the bloodshed occurred abroad, Norfolk very quickly found itself on the front line. On 3 November 1914 three German battlecruisers and three cruisers fired on Great Yarmouth, making the county the first to be shelled from the sea during the war. Coastal patrols were started, not only in response to naval attacks but also concerns of a possible invasion. The Germans also set about laying mines off the east coast and attacking shipping by U-boats, which heavily disrupted Norfolk's vital fishing industry.

In addition to the naval threat, the First World War introduced a new danger of attack from the skies. German airships, or Zeppelins, penetrated into East Anglia at night and Norfolk suffered the first fatal bombing raid of the war. The first bombs to be dropped on British soil were on the north coast at Sheringham, during a Zeppelin raid on 18 January 1915. Bombs were also dropped on King's

Lynn, Great Yarmouth and their surrounding villages. Thereafter, Zeppelins were to be a regular sight passing over Norfolk's air space and frequently dropped their bombs on the county.

Warfare serves to stimulate innovation in military technology and the Great War was no exception, ushering in new types of fighting machines. Norfolk participated in developments in air warfare involving Britain's own aeroplanes and airships. The Royal Flying Corps had forty-seven airfields across the county. Airships were based at Pulham St Mary in South Norfolk from 1915. The Royal Navy Air Service established a station there, from which airships patrolled the North Sea. In relation to land warfare, it was at the Elveden Estate in Breckland, in 1916, where the first tanks were tested before going into combat in France.

More than sixty auxiliary hospitals were established in the county to accommodate soldiers recovering from injuries and surgery. These were set up in some of the large halls and houses and run by the British Red Cross and the Order of St John.

THE NORFOLK REGIMENT ABROAD

The Norfolk Regiment were engaged in hostilities across all theatres, fielding twenty battalions. The 8th Battalion fought in France and was present at the Battle of the Somme, where they reached the German trenches on the first day of engagement. In all, 32,375 men fought for the regiment during the Great War, of whom 5,576 were killed; one third at the Somme. The 2nd Battalion fought in Mesopotamia and the two territorial battalions served at Gallipoli.

At Gallipoli, the 5th Norfolks became 'the vanished battalion'. Having taken part in the attack on Turkish positions, they were last seen advancing into a burning wood. They were never seen nor heard of again. The missing included a number of royal servants from the Sandringham estate.

A graphic record of the regiment's participation in the Great War is preserved in a unique document; the Casualty Book. It records details of more than 15,000 soldiers between the outbreak of war in 1914 and their return home in 1919. The book was compiled at the Britannia Barracks in Norwich, where the regiment was based. As information about casualties arrived back in Britain, regimental clerks transcribed the details. Each entry contains a soldier's name, service number, battalion, details of their wound, injury or sickness, and the hospital that they were sent to, as well as those who were killed in action. The book, which is now in the care of the Royal Norfolk Regimental Museum at Norwich Castle, provides us with a unique insight into a typical infantry unit of the British army at that time.

Edith Cavell (1865–1915) is a famous Norfolk name associated with the Great War, who showed extreme bravery and selfless dedication to saving human life in the face of oppression. Edith was born at Swardeston, near Norwich, and travelled to Belgium at the start of the war. At great personal risk, over a period of nine months, she sheltered British soldiers during the German occupation and assisted nearly 200 British, French and Belgians to escape to the Netherlands. She was eventually arrested and found guilty of treason. Sentenced to death, her execution by firing squad received international condemnation. She was eventually buried at Norwich Cathedral. Edith's memory has lived on for her self-sacrifice in the face of tyranny. Her name joins other great Norfolk characters, including Boudica and Robert Kett, each of whom were prepared to take a stand against forces of oppression.

THE END OF THE WAR

The First World War ended on the eleventh day of the eleventh month, 1918. The loss of human life that it had suffered over the four years changed the face of Norfolk. Many of those who did return suffered from a range of injuries and disabilities. This was a pattern that was replicated right across the country.

It was in response to the scale of suffering and loss of life that the author H.G. Wells prophesied that the 1914–18 conflict would be 'the war that would end war'. Sadly, the words of Marshal Foch, French general and Supreme Allied Commander, were to be more accurate, describing the end of what was to be referred to as the Great War as 'not a peace, it is an armistice for twenty years'.

NORFOLK BETWEEN THE WORLD WARS

The years 1918–39 provided a brief respite, in which there was a renewed sense of hope that war on such a scale between civilised nations would not be repeated. There was an initial climate of optimism to improve the lot of the post-war generation. Norfolk had lost large numbers of mainly young men who had been sent abroad to fight and the county, as elsewhere, had to adjust to a new era in new ways.

The peace of 1918 initially brought a worldwide economic boom; a period during which working conditions did steadily improve. Wages had increased for many during wartime and expectations increased for better living conditions. Working hours were reduced and workers received paid holidays. A new house-building programme was started and there were improvements in public health and life expectancy.

New forms of popular entertainment were embraced by an eager population. Cinema was introduced and people bought wireless sets, both of which developed a mass following. These new media also became important vehicles for the dissemination of news and information throughout the rest of the century. The war also accelerated the influence of American popular culture in Europe. New musical crazes included jazz and ragtime. The decade after the war became known as the Roaring Twenties.

Norfolk was reinvigorated by improved communications. The early years of the twentieth century had seen the expansion of the railways. In turn, the railways served to stimulate the development of the tourism industry, connecting Norfolk not only with London but establishing links with Birmingham and the east Midlands. It was at this time that the Broads grew in popularity as a tourist area, in tandem with seaside resorts. The establishment of local buses in the 1920s improved the lot of agricultural communities. Norwich also had a tram system that lasted into the 1930s.

The 1930s was a period of economic depression, with many farmers falling into bankruptcy and their land bought up at very low prices. Farms now favoured the increased use of the tractor over traditional horse-based agriculture and the labour force declined during these years.

In Breckland, the agricultural slump gave way to a new form of land use. This has historically been a marginal land, with poor soils and harsh climate. Its landscape of heathland and rabbit warrens had become dominated by large estates. Following the First World War, social changes, combined with low agricultural potential, saw the estates and their farms fall out of use. The Forestry Commission began to acquire the land and established what is now known as Thetford Forest, where they started planting trees in 1922. A completely new landscape was created with blocks of pine woodland, which now characterise the approach to Norfolk by road. The original purpose was to create a resource of timber for the nation although today it also serves a role as a forest parkland in its own right.

Further east, a sugar beet factory was constructed at Cantley in 1912, which was just the second in the country. In 1920, the industry expanded and it became a national processing plant. Today it remains one of only four such centres in the country.

In Norwich, the striking new City Hall was constructed between 1932 and 1938 and was described by Pevsner as 'the foremost English public building of between the wars'. It was designed in the Art Deco style, with grand frontal colonnade. Its grand opening was presided over by King George VI and Queen Elizabeth.

Norwich's core industries, including the engineering works at Boulton and Paul and Laurence and Scott, survived the Great Depression. However, the inter-war years saw more stagnation at Great Yarmouth, with King's Lynn faring a little better. At Thetford, Burrells' business declined, resulting from the rise of smaller vehicles that used the internal combustion engine. At their height, Burrells' works had occupied much of the centre of Thetford. Today, just one building from the former works survives, situated in Minstergate, now housing a museum of the company.

Norfolk's changing farming practices had a knock-on effect on the smaller towns, which had traditionally been associated with servicing local agricultural needs and providing rural markets. Several suffered a decline in population while others managed to develop a new industrial base, which reflected the changing needs of the economy and population.

East Dereham was the main market town, situated at 'the heart of Norfolk'. Its central location favoured a developing role as a railway junction. Its earlier agricultural function was steadily replaced by small industries, including engineering and cabinet making. Other small towns such as Swaffham, that continued to rely heavily on their agricultural market function, suffered a decline.

One of Norfolk's more famous citizens of the inter-war years was Henry Blogg, a lifeboatman at Cromer. Henry was to become the most decorated lifeboatman in the history of the RNLI. His numerous awards included the Empire Gallantry Medal (1924), the British Empire Medal and the George Cross (1941). He also received a silver medal for rescuing thirty men in 1932 and a gold watch for a rescue on the notorious Happisburgh Sands.

Another significant event in the history of both Norfolk and the nation occurred during these years. The longest ever strike began at the unlikely location of Burston School, situated near Diss in south Norfolk. The strike lasted for an astonishing twenty-five years, from 1914 to 1939, following the dismissal of two teachers, Kitty Higdon and her husband Thomas. Both were Christian socialists and became concerned about the illegal employment of local children and general school conditions, which led to arguments with their managers. The Norfolk Education Committee responded by offering the Higdons the choice of working elsewhere or dismissal. On 1 April

1914 their pupils went on strike in support of the pair. The strike was to become a focus for both the Trades Union movement and the Labour Party. An annual rally is still held in the village to commemorate the event, organised by the Transport and General Workers' Union, on the first Sunday every September.

THE OUTBREAK OF THE SECOND WORLD WAR

The Armistice of 1918 achieved peace on the Western Front but elsewhere instability and significant unrest had been set in motion across Europe, Russia, the former Ottoman Empire and China. Germany remained strong and her people maintained a deep resentment for the terms imposed in the Treaty of Versailles. There was a steady escalation of global violence. In 1928 Japanese forces took control in Manchuria. In 1935 the Italian fascist dictator Mussolini attacked Abyssinia. In Germany, Adolf Hitler became head of a coalition government and in 1933, instigated the rise of the Nazis. In 1936 Hitler sent troops into the Rhineland and in 1938 into Austria. Following German entry into Poland, Britain declared war with Germany on 3 September 1939.

Norfolk once again stood in a vulnerable position in relation to a possible invasion and may well have found itself in the front line of any such attack. Defences were set up both around the coast and across lines of communication further inland. The spectre of invasion was to remain until 1942.

For civilians, there was an immediate impact. Piles of sandbags to protect property appeared in the streets. Blackout regulations were imposed on towns at night to avoid them being seen by enemy aircraft. Food was stockpiled and people were issued with gas masks in readiness for an attack. Food rationing was imposed and a black market in provisions quickly arose.

At the start of the war, children and vulnerable people were evacuated from locations considered to be in most danger. The evacuees were billeted on people in rural areas, including Norfolk. Later, it was decided to evacuate children from within a 10-mile strip along the east coast. This involved the movement of Norfolk's own youngsters further inland and beyond, to homes in the Midlands.

Civilians were keen to do whatever they could to aid the war effort. The Supermarine Spitfire came to symbolise the defiant response of the British people against Nazi Germany. From 1940 'Spitfire Funds' were collected by communities to build more of the fighter aircraft. In Norwich, the artist Phillipa Miller and her sister Pamela built a miniature house of 1930s' style from cardboard and scraps of what were then scarce materials (even wood was in short supply in wartime Britain). They exhibited the model locally and used it to steadily raise funds towards the cost of a new Spitfire for the war effort. 'Spitfire Cottage' has survived and is now exhibited at the Museum of Norwich.

THE HOME FRONT

Preparations to counter a possible invasion were put in place. The Home Guard was formed. Some of the First World War pillboxes were reused and others constructed at strategic locations in relation to airfields, key communication routes, industrial sites and around the coast. The coastal belt became a first line of defence and the beaches were mined. Norwich was designated the command centre for the defence of the whole of East Anglia. The city was defended by its own pill-boxes, roadblocks and anti-tank defences.

Meanwhile, the Air Ministry sought to outwit the German military offensive by creating a series of decoy sites. Dummy airfields were constructed on heathland, such as Kelling, and on disused First World War airstrips. Props were used to create the impression of runways, bomb dumps and fuel stores from the air. They were set up around strategic locations, such as the port of Great Yarmouth, to divert the enemy's attention.

In 1939 Norfolk had five operational airfields. Over the next five years many more were constructed. The county was chosen for this special role due to its proximity to the Continent and its predominantly flat landscape. By 1944 it contained thirty-seven airfields.

RAF personnel who flew from Norfolk include the television personality Raymond Baxter (1922–2006), famous to a generation for presenting the science programme *Tomorrow's World* between 1965 and 1977, who served in the RAF with distinction. Baxter was based at RAF Coltishall in 1945, flying a Spitfire XVI.

The needs of the war drove the local economy, especially through the influx of thousands of service people, including those associated with the airfields. Army camps too were located right across the countryside. In spite of the bombing, local engineering firms such as Boulton & Paul in Norwich and Savage's at King's Lynn continued to be busy. Norfolk's textile firms were engaged in the production of service uniforms and even the manufacture of parachutes.

Agricultural production became more important once again and was given a boost with the rise of mechanisation. Norfolk's wheat production reached record levels. While men joined the forces, volunteers of the Women's Land Army undertook the full range of jobs that had been undertaken by men. The new recruits became adept at ploughing, harvesting, care of livestock and milking.

At sea, the coastal fishing industry was badly affected. German E-boats (fast patrol boats) lurked offshore to take out convoy vessels, particularly in the zone between the Happisburgh Sands and the coast. Floating magnetic mines were an additional hazard. In order to counter the threat to coastal shipping, motor torpedo boats of the Royal Navy operated from Great Yarmouth. The RNLI also played an important role throughout.

Land to the north of Thetford was taken over by the War Office as a military training area, where the Stanford Training Area was established in 1942. The 7th Armoured Division, famously nicknamed the 'Desert Rats', were stationed there from January to May 1944 in order to prepare for the invasion of Normandy. It is still in use by the British Army today.

FIGHTING THE WAR

Norwich suffered badly from heavy bombing by the Luftwaffe, the German air force, during the Second World War, initially experiencing attacks in 1940. In March of 1942 the RAF undertook a large-scale bombing raid on the historic Hanseatic port of Lübeck. Hitler was furious at this destruction and chose to respond by selectively bombing English cultural targets, which were chosen from the Baedeker guidebook. The 'Baedeker raids' targeted Norwich, along with other historic English cities including Canterbury, York, Bath and Exeter.

The severity of the bombing during April 1942 transformed the face of Norwich. High explosive and incendiary attacks between the 27th and 29th left 231 civilians dead and nearly 700 injured. Over 3,000 houses were damaged and a number of churches were destroyed, along with many shops and businesses. The raids caused prolonged disruption and over 100 factories were lost, including Cuthberts Printing Works, Morgan's Brewery and Caley's chocolate factory. The railway stations also suffered damage.

Norwich continued to suffer air raids through to 1943. Great Yarmouth was also targeted and much of the surviving medieval town was destroyed. Then, in 1944, the county was subjected to attacks from the V1 flying bombs, known as 'doodlebugs', and from V2 rockets.

One lesser-known military facility that operated in the county was Beeston Hill 'Y Station', at Sheringham. This was a listening station for intercepting German wireless transmissions from E-boats and U-boats. Beeston was part of a chain of stations that forwarded messages to Bletchley Park, where enemy communications were monitored and countered. Beeston played a vital role in the protection of Allied shipping and especially in the Battle of the Atlantic.

The Norfolk Regiment became the Royal Norfolk Regiment on 3 June 1935. In the Second World War they raised seven active service battalions, from which more than 2,000 men were killed over the five-year period. They operated in theatres across the globe. Five men were awarded the highest award for bravery, the Victoria Cross.

One battalion was nearly destroyed at Dunkirk in 1940. The 2nd Battalion of the Norfolk Regiment were part of the British Expeditionary Force and suffered heavy losses, with just 139 survivors from 1,000 men. In one particular episode, ninety prisoners were executed by the German SS.

Others faced captivity following the fall of Singapore. In February 1942, three Territorial battalions were present at the surrender and most were sent to work on the notorious railway through the jungle of Thailand, and were subjected to appalling conditions.

In March 1944 the Japanese launched an offensive in Burma in advance of a planned assault on India. The 2nd Royal Norfolks were sent from India to reinforce the garrison at Kohima. This became one of the bloodiest and most savage battles of the entire war. The garrison showed extreme bravery, none more so than Captain John Randle, who won the VC by charging a Japanese gun emplacement, tragically dying in the process.

RECORDING THE EVENTS

Some local artists were able to provide a unique view of events. John Craske (1881–1943) was born at Sheringham and in his early days worked as a fisherman. He was diagnosed with a benign brain tumour and, as his health deteriorated, he turned to stitching pictures. Craske created an extraordinary embroidery depicting the evacuation of Allied soldiers from the beaches of Dunkirk, when the British Expeditionary Force had been surrounded by the German army. 'The Evacuation from Dunkirk', held at Norwich Castle Museum, was produced during the time of Craske's acute mental illness. It has been recognised how the process of undertaking hand-stitched work can provide a coping mechanism during times of stress and can be a form of therapy for those suffering from mental anguish. Craske described his style as 'painting in wools'.

Philippa Miller (1905–2006) was a Norwich artist who worked during the war as a teacher by day and for the rescue services by night. She painted dozens of wartime scenes in the city, all based on her personal observations. She recorded dramatic events while they were still fresh in her mind. In addition to her paintings and sketches, Miller provided a vivid insight into life in wartime Norfolk through her writings. She described the contrast between living in the idyllic setting of the Norfolk Broads and the uncertainty of daily life in the city and along the east coast, which was subjected to bombing raids by the German Luftwaffe and destruction from the V1 flying bombs.

'OVER HERE' – THE FRIENDLY INVASION

Norfolk and East Anglia more generally were at the forefront of the air war offensive, which was to swing the tide of the war firmly in favour of the Allies against Nazi Germany. In 1942 the aircraft of Bomber Command operating in Norfolk were joined by those of the American Eighth Airforce. Airbases were established across the county and some 100,000 acres of Norfolk farmland were taken over by the US Army Air Force (USAAF). The USAAF went on to establish strong ties with the villages of East Anglia, which have lasted to the present day. At this pivotal period in world history, Norfolk and its immediately surrounding counties resembled a massive aircraft carrier from which the air offensive on Hitler's Third Reich was launched. American airbases were situated right across the county, as well as in Suffolk, Cambridgeshire and Lincolnshire. The iconic aircraft that flew from Norfolk included the B-17 Flying Fortress and B-24 Liberator. Norwich itself was ringed by airfields flying the Liberator bombers.

Not only was Norfolk's resident population temporarily inflated by the arrival of military personnel, but the presence of these airbases reminds us yet again of its international dimension. It was the county's peripheral location that left it best placed to station bombers attacking the Continent.

Most of the serving airmen were very young, mostly between just 17 and 21 years of age. Some of the individuals were well known for their previous careers and brought further attention to the region. They included some famous names. The Hollywood actor James Stewart (1908–97), star of such movies as *Vertigo* and numerous westerns, was a captain and operations officer for the 703rd Bomb Squadron and was posted to Tibenham airbase in November 1943. In March 1944 he was transferred to the 453rd Bombardment Group at Old Buckenham. Throughout his career, Stewart flew as lead pilot in B-24 Liberators.

Another Hollywood actor, Walter Matthau (1920–2000), who starred in *The Odd Couple*, served in the Eighth Air Force. As a radioman-gunner aboard a Liberator, he served in the same 453rd Bombardment Group as Stewart, also based at Old Buckenham.

A surviving example of an American airbase is at the small village of Thorpe Abbotts near Diss. Here, the injection of service personnel outnumbered the villagers and had a massive impact on the community. Even today, locals continue to relate stories of those now distant times. The 100th Bomb Group stationed there had a reputation for sustaining unusually heavy losses, flying their B-17 Flying Fortresses, and were referred to as the 'Bloody Hundredth'. Between June 1943 and April 1945, they lost 177 aircraft and 732 airmen. Today, Thorpe Abbotts airbase has been preserved as a museum and memorial to the brave aircrews and also as an educational resource for the current generation.

The legacy of the Second World War airfields in Norfolk has left its mark across the county as what have been termed 'ghost fields'. Today, only RAF Marham remains in front-line operation. The station at Horsham St Faith has become today's commercial Norwich Airport. While Thorpe Abbotts has been preserved in its capacity as a museum, sadly the others remain in varying states of decay.

THE LAST STAGES OF THE WAR AND THE RETURN TO PEACE

In June 1944 the 1st Battalion of the Royal Norfolks was present at D-Day. Two battalions took part in the subsequent assaults on Caen and Falaise. The 1st Battalion continued in the vanguard of the drive eastwards through France, Belgium, Holland and into Germany, leading to the liberation of Europe. In Burma, the 2nd Royal Norfolks continued the fight against the Japanese. Back home, prisoner of war camps were set up across the county and the wider region to receive large numbers of prisoners taken during the final stages of the war.

The war in Europe ended on 8 May 1945 and victory against Japan was declared on 15 August. Norfolk was left exhausted and in need of investment, reconstruction and renewed infrastructure. Together with the whole country, it looked to recovery, towards an age of sustained peace and a place in a Britain and Europe of renewed growth and prosperity.

11

MODERN TIMES

1945 to the Present

When Victory in Europe was declared, the people of the county came together to celebrate the end of six long years of war. Accounts tell of how crowds thronged the streets of Norwich and Liberator aircraft from the American air-bases flew overhead alongside RAF Mosquitoes, adding to the festivities by dropping coloured flares, whilst being illuminated in columns of light by the city's searchlights. Following Japan's subsequent surrender, the initial period of euphoria and aspiration for the future quickly gave way to a decade of realism.

Post-war Britain became a period of even deeper austerity than had been faced during the preceding six years. The war had already drained the country and reparations left it on the verge of bankruptcy. However, under the new Labour government, with its vision of a 'New Jerusalem', Britain looked forward to progressive new policies that included the introduction of the National Health Service, the Welfare State, and a major house-building programme.

On the international stage, a new political world order emerged, with two superpowers, the United States and the Soviet Union. The years between 1945 and 1990 are known as the Cold War. Norfolk once again found itself on the front line, this time of a very different type of conflict and being strategically positioned in relation to threats from Russia and continental Europe.

While the global impact of the confrontation was one of conflict and instability at many flashpoints around the globe, western Europe, in contrast, was to experience an unprecedented period of peace and stability, eventually leading to years of prosperity. In the West, this became a time of sustained economic growth, higher wages, shorter working weeks, improved health care and greater access to education. But people were also now hungry for change and there was a reaction across society against the old social order and establishment. The 1960s ushered in a cultural revolution across music and the arts, with strong new influences introduced from America and Europe. In 1973 Britain joined the European Union and in 1994 the Channel Tunnel opened, creating a physical link to the Continent.

BUILDING A NEW NORFOLK

Post-war Norfolk was faced with many immediate problems. Wartime had seen the influx of thousands of military personnel, especially at the airbases, but, at the end of hostilities, most of them had moved away within a year of the war's end. This sudden withdrawal of so many people had a massive impact locally. The resident population was left alone to rebuild the county after the war damage it had sustained, especially in the main towns. There was an immediate shortage of both labour and funds to undertake the job. Yet, the visual face of urban Norfolk was to be transformed as the impact of the Second World War was addressed.

The local economy had been geared toward servicing the needs of the country in wartime and it needed to develop in new ways. The post-war economy maintained a focus on agriculture but also diversified further into other areas of food production, food processing and associated industries. There was also a steady emphasis on developing the tourism sector, which was centred on, and gave a boost to, some of the more deprived coastal areas.

A further consideration in the reconstruction of the county was to appreciate historical differences between its different sub-regions, especially between the east and west. Both have often developed independently and at a different pace, at stages throughout history. In terms of prosperity, King's Lynn in the west and Norwich and Great Yarmouth in the east have remained prominent since their original foundation but in the south, Thetford has never fully regained its early importance, despite its position as a gateway into the county.

NORFOLK IN THE COLD WAR

A precarious international balance of power existed throughout the period of the Cold War, which involved the creation of strategic defences based on the principle of a deterrent threat of nuclear weapons. At times, the world came perilously close to nuclear destruction, most notably during the Cuban Missile Crisis of 1962. Norfolk's airfields are a reminder of its strategic location and international military importance in the nuclear age. RAF Swanton Morley was in service from 1942 until 1995 and RAF Coltishall from 1938 to 2006. RAF Marham, which had opened in 1916, was home to the V bombers and tankers that were the spearhead of the deterrent. Together with nearby Lakenheath and Mildenhall in Suffolk, these bases formed an important part of NATO's strategic air defence.

On the ground, in 1959 the Royal Norfolks were amalgamated with the Suffolk Regiment to become part of the 1st East Anglian Regiment; later part of the Royal Anglian Regiment. They participated in campaigns across the world including in Korea, Cyprus and Aden. From 1970 the 1st Battalion, The Royal Anglian Regiment served in Northern Ireland.

A CHANGING WORLD

The 1950s and '60s gave rise to new social attitudes within a changing world. Post-war depression was replaced by a wave of rising optimism and excitement. At the same time, there was a reaction against the perceived complacency of the old political class and anti-establishment movements grew up.

Young people who had lived through depressed years were looking for a good time and a new youth culture emerged. Some more aggressive elements included the Mods and Rockers, who became notorious visitors to Norfolk's east coast, especially to Great Yarmouth. Trouble first flared up in 1964, when a spate of unsociable behaviour led to confrontations on the seafronts. In the following years they invaded on a regular basis throughout the summer and at weekends, often clashing in public areas.

COMMUNICATIONS

Norfolk's physical isolation from other parts of the country was an obstacle to the pace of post-war change. It suffered further reduction in its transport capability when much of the railway infrastructure was removed through the reshaping of British Railways in 1963–65 under Dr Beeching, who was the first Chairman of the British Railways Board. These cutbacks resulted in the removal of the direct rail line linking east and west Norfolk and restricted travel across the county.

Communications between Norfolk and the rest of the country remained slow, and the county experienced a sense of isolation. Long drives were needed to reach other parts. The nearest city beyond the county is Cambridge, 65 miles from Norwich, which is still a long journey on roads lacking motorways.

Many of Norfolk's residents felt that this isolation was a blessing in disguise; contributing to the quality of life by slowing down the pace of change. However, demands of the economy and a growing population required modernisation and better connections beyond the county.

Communications have improved significantly, particularly since the 1990s, with dual carriageway links southward, through Suffolk and on to London. Improved rail services have enabled regular train journeys to London in under two hours and an occasional ninety-minute service started in 2019.

Today, air transport provides new benefits to the economy, connecting Norwich with the North Sea gas fields and business worldwide and for tourism. Norwich International Airport provides a one-hour connection to the major international air hub at Amsterdam Schiphol, helping to connect the county with other parts of the world.

THE LAND

There was a revival in Norfolk's agriculture after 1945. New farming techniques started to be introduced following the end of the war. In particular, mechanisation quickly replaced the remnants of horse power. The appearance of the landscape altered, although perhaps not aesthetically improved, with hedgerows removed and fields opened up. Norfolk's modern agriculture is now dominated by cereal production. The agricultural sector remains of prime importance, with strong linkages to retail and to food processing, which is served by a number of famous national brands.

The name Colman's remains synonymous with Norwich and Norfolk. The company continues to be a major regional employer. Turkey farming was introduced on an intensive scale by Bernard Matthews, who was farming ten million birds in the mid-1990s. Many other companies have been engaged in food processing, while sugarbeet production, another important employer, is centred at Cantley in the east and King's Lynn in the west.

In the south, Thetford Forest has become the largest area of pine woodland in lowland Britain. This artificially created landscape has transformed Breckland into a highly distinctive landscape that characterises the southern border of Norfolk and signals entry into the county.

Despite the predominantly advantageous natural climate, Norfolk's east coast, particularly to the north of Great Yarmouth, remains vulnerable to extreme weather conditions. The area has been subjected to flooding for centuries and there have been dreadful floods within living memory. Overnight on 31 January 1953, 100 people on Norfolk's east coast were killed when a high spring tide and windstorm combined to produce an abnormal and lethal storm tide.

NORFOLK'S INDUSTRIES

In addition to agriculture, Norfolk's leading industrial sectors are tourism, engineering, business and financial services, and the offshore industry. A famous Norfolk company associated with motor engineering is Lotus Cars. In 1966 the company and associated racing team created by Colin Chapman relocated from Herefordshire to Hethel in Norfolk. The site was built during 1942 as an RAF base, used by the US Air Force. The runway and access roads were to form the basis of their test track. Lotus Cars is still based at this site.

The county has a strong track record of attracting film-makers for location shooting. Some of the more famous films shot in Norfolk include *The Dam Busters* (1954), *The Go-Between* (1971), *The Eagle Has Landed* (1976), *Revolution* (1985), *Out of Africa* (1985), *Full Metal Jacket* (1987), *Shakespeare in Love* (1999), *Die Another Day* (2002), *Stardust* (2007), *Atonement* (2007) and *The Duchess* (2008), together with TV series including *Dad's Army* (1968–77), *'Allo 'Allo* (1982–92), *David Copperfield* (2000) and *Kingdom* (2007–09).

There was a long-standing association between the TV series *Dad's Army* and the town of Thetford. Set in the fictional location of Warmington-on-Sea, most of the external location filming was done around Thetford. The cast and crew were regular guests of the town, where they came to stay each summer for the location work. The town now hosts its own *Dad's Army* museum.

The North Sea has provided a major boost to the county's economy through the offshore industry. Exploration in the early 1960s discovered oil and gas, bringing new and significant benefits. As the energy fields were opened up, Great Yarmouth developed into the largest offshore marine base in Europe, to support this industry. A terminal was constructed at Bacton, in the north-east, and gas began to be piped there from the Leman Field in 1968. Bacton currently handles a third of the UK's total gas supply. Oil started to be piped ashore in 1975, from the massive fields, which included Brent and Alpha. Today, there are some 350 companies located in and around Great Yarmouth that are engaged with the offshore industry.

Norfolk and Norwich are well served through two universities; the University of East Anglia (UEA), established in 1963, and Norwich University of the Arts (NUA), which was founded over 170 years ago by the artists of the Norwich School of Artists. Norwich Research Park is a leading centre for innovation and is considered to be one of Europe's leading centres for research into biotechnology, the environment, food and health, all of which are key areas for the future of mankind in the twenty-first century.

LIVING IN NORFOLK TODAY

Today, Norfolk is renowned for its beautiful natural environment and quality of life. It combines the benefits of being a rural area with a vibrant economy, flourishing businesses and new industries, and is a centre of innovation. It is close to mainland Europe and valued as a hub of culture and heritage. It is a desirable holiday destination and north Norfolk is a popular location for second homes.

The main urban centres continue to be the historic towns of Norwich, King's Lynn, Great Yarmouth and Thetford. Norwich is regarded as both the county and regional capital. Important for its industry and as a commercial centre, it is also appreciated as the cultural capital of East Anglia.

It is the centre for administration, a range of services and regional media.

Great Yarmouth is the second largest urban centre in Norfolk. Its historically important fishing industry has been extinguished since 1945 through foreign intervention and the introduction of industrial fishing. This decline has changed the character of the town. Most of the medieval Rows were finally destroyed by Hitler's air raids. Sadly, the town was deprived of the scale of post-war investment seen at other damaged British urban centres. Today, Great Yarmouth is important for port-related activities, as well as serving the offshore oil and gas industry. An ambitious Outer Harbour project began in 2007 and has continued to attract further investment and development. Yarmouth is the third largest holiday resort in the country and the hub for visits to the Norfolk Broads.

King's Lynn is the third largest centre. Its commerce is centred on the modern docks and its industrial estates. Manufacturing industries again include food processing. It has maintained its two regular historic markets and is an important regional arts venue. Lynn retains a richness of architecture, with some very special survivals from earlier centuries. Other centres in west Norfolk are the seaside town of Hunstanton and the market town of Downham Market.

Thetford experienced post-war growth that has been boosted by the process of London overspill; a scheme that saw residents of Greater London move away from the capital to establish new communities and industry across south-east England. Thetford is a distribution centre and the focal location on the main route into the county from London and the south, and just 30 miles from Cambridge. It is the home to a number of manufacturing companies.

Norfolk's single city and three largest towns are supported by its network of smaller market towns in between, which continue to provide housing, services and employment for their surrounding rural areas. These all have a distinctive character, reflecting their local regions.

The royal connection through the Sandringham Estate in west Norfolk is held in special affection by the people of the county. Sandringham has been the private home for four generations of British monarchs. King George V (r. 1910–36) called it 'the place I love better than anywhere else in the world'. Today's royal family spend the winter months there and it is where the Queen broadcasts to the nation each Christmas. The late Diana, Princess of Wales, was born at Park House near the church and grew up on the Sandringham Estate. Sandringham today is a popular tourist destination, attracting visitors from across the country and abroad.

TOURISM AND LEISURE

Tourism has now become the largest single industry sector in Norfolk. It increasingly supports employment, accounting for 65,400 jobs in 2017, which was 18.4 per cent of all employment in the county. In the same year it also contributed £3.2 billion to the local economy.

The traditional focus of tourist activity has been concentrated on the coastal resorts, centring on Great Yarmouth in the east, Cromer and Sheringham in the north, and Hunstanton in the west, as well as in Norwich and the Broads. Today the offer embraces more diverse attractions, including a range of leisure activities, museums, castles and historic buildings, stately homes, sports, zoos, leisure parks and heritage railways.

THE ARTS AND POPULAR CULTURE

Norwich and Norfolk are a vibrant centre for the arts and with a strong heritage commitment. There are around ninety museums in the county. The flagship organisation is Norfolk Museums Service, which was created in 1974 and comprises a network of ten museums that reflect the county's geographical sub-regions and their communities. The Sainsbury Centre for Visual Arts is also a museum and art gallery, opened in 1978 on the campus of UEA, with award-winning buildings designed by Norman Foster and Wendy Cheesman.

Norfolk's long tradition as a home for writers, spanning the years from Julian of Norwich to Sir Andrew Motion (Poet Laureate 1999–2009), paved the way for Norwich to make a successful bid in 2012 to become designated England's first UNESCO City of Literature; a home to writers, thinkers and storytellers.

Many artists have lived and worked in Norfolk in the years since the Second World War. Prominent names include Michael Andrews (1928–95) and Colin Self (b. 1941), while numerous others have left a significant mark. Hallam Ashley (1900–87) was a photographer of East Anglian subjects whose pictures have featured in exhibitions around the world. His work is evocative of earlier twentieth-century life across Britain. He has left a delightful record of the rural lifestyle and trades that characterised Norfolk and Suffolk at that time.

Another artist worthy of note is John Moray-Smith (1888–1958), who has been described as an eccentric genius. Moray-Smith created three-dimensional panels depicting episodes from Norfolk's past and themes relating to its social history. Many of his works were displayed in local pubs, where they could be enjoyed by ordinary people. A number of these quirky works can still be seen in different parts of the county, including some in museums and others still surviving as fittings in pubs.

SPORT

Norfolk plays host to a wide range of top sports. Norwich City Football Club has been at the heart of Norfolk's community since its foundation in 1902. Unlike the situation in most cities and other parts of Britain, they enjoy support from the whole county and also across the wider region. Their first home was at Newmarket Road, until 1908, when they moved to 'The Nest', in Rosary Road, nestling in the space vacated by a disused quarry. The name of the ground was in keeping with both the nickname, 'the Canaries', and with the shape of the ground as a bird's nest.

The club moved to its current home at Carrow Road in 1935, following promotion to Division 2. The Canaries first won promotion to the top (First) Division in 1972. They have won the League Cup twice, in 1962 and 1985. They enjoy a long-standing rivalry with their East Anglian neighbours Ipswich Town. The song sung by fans 'On the Ball City' is recognised as the oldest football song anywhere in the world.

There is horseracing at Great Yarmouth and Fakenham and greyhound racing at Great Yarmouth and Swaffham. Popular motor sports include speedway in King's Lynn and motor racing at Snetterton. There is also a strong tradition of boxing in the county.

Norfolk's waterways provide extensive opportunities for boating, with sailing and yachting on the Broads and at the coast. Holiday cruising on the Broads, centred at Wroxham, is a popular tourist attraction.

ARCHAEOLOGY IN NORFOLK

There has been a nationwide boom in the discipline of archaeology since the 1970s, resulting in a transformation of our understanding of the past. In 1974 Norfolk was the first county in Britain to create a county archaeological unit. At around the same time, it was becoming recognised that the majority of new archaeological discoveries were being made by amateur enthusiasts, especially those employing new technology in the form of metal detectors. Norfolk's archaeologists subsequently gained a reputation for working closely with metal detector users to maximise recorded information about these new finds. This approach was aggressively criticised beyond the county borders, supposedly for encouraging what was termed 'the looting of our past'. But since the mid-1990s, the 'Norfolk System' of proactive liaison with detectorists has become adopted on a national basis, within the national Portable Antiquities Scheme.

The Norfolk approach has resulted in more archaeological finds being recorded than in any other part of Britain. In particular, the largest number of Britain's discoveries classified as 'Treasure' come from the county, accounting for around 12 per cent of all national cases (currently in the region of 130 each year). As a result of this proliferation of finds, it has often been a temptation to overemphasise the significance of Norfolk's historic role.

It has long been a question as to whether, and when, Norfolk's extraordinarily large volume of archaeological finds reflects genuinely significant events. The system of reporting finds, together with the large amounts of agricultural land available for metal detecting, undoubtedly contribute to the above normal number of discoveries. The result may sometimes lead us to infer an exaggerated importance of a site or time period.

However, it is clear that Norfolk has always played a role in the unfolding history of England, even if it has not always been a central one. Its geographical position as a borderland or edgeland has often defined this role, on the periphery but still engaged in national events.

THE FUTURE

Modern Norfolk has become a relatively quieter part of England, maintaining a balance between preserving its natural beauty, alongside encouraging new industries and technological innovation. But the twenty-first century is posing new challenges. The delicate balance between sustaining the environment and providing the services needed by the growing population is being challenged. The natural world is under threat as never before and Norfolk's coastline, with its soft geology, continues to face quickening erosion by the North Sea. A rapid expansion in home building, with accompanying road developments, is causing massive pressure in and around the towns and villages to encroach on sensitive locations and agricultural land. Today's developments could potentially change the character of the county and make its towns and most beautiful locations unrecognisable.

Energy needs are growing and wind power has been characterised as an ecologically friendly form for the future. Offshore wind farms have already been established around Norfolk's long coastline at Wells, Great Yarmouth and Sheringham Shoals. Now, some of the world's biggest wind farms are planned for the future around Norfolk's coast. Not only will they supply the energy needs of the rural population and beyond but the growing industry will also be a source of skilled jobs and attract other financial investment. But there will again be some cost and a balance to be struck in terms of impact on the coastline and local countryside, its population and wildlife.

In addition to the threatened encroachment into the rural environment, the future of Norfolk's historic legacy is also under threat. Its surviving churches and other ancient buildings are costly to maintain and many are now being used for purposes not always sympathetic to their historic significance. Concerns over the intrusion of high-rise constructions on the cityscape of Norwich, together with the disappearance of familiar historic buildings, are live current issues. Local organisations including the Norfolk Archaeological Trust and the Norwich Society are leading the way with initiatives to preserve the historic past, including preservation by acquisition and active engagement with the legal planning process.

Norfolk is recognised as a great place to live and to visit. It lies beneath big skies, with diverse landscapes ranging from the spectacular white- and red-banded cliffs at Hunstanton, through marshes at Cley and Thornham, the Broads at Hickling, Ranworth and Wroxham, and the billiard-table-flat Fenland and Wash in the far west, with its murmurations of seabirds. It is a county of great beaches with endless stretches of golden sand at Holkham, Wells-next-the-Sea, Holme, Great Yarmouth and Brancaster. A star cast of great houses at Blickling, Houghton, Felbrigg, Oxborough, Holkham and Sandringham is accompanied by other historic locations, including the atmospheric Castle Acre, Castle Rising and abundant medieval buildings at King's Lynn. Beautiful destination towns include Holt and Burnham Market, within a landscape interspersed with castles, round-towered churches and windmills. Surviving ancient archaeological sites include Seahenge, Grimes Graves, Caistor Roman Town and Burgh Castle; all nationally recognised in their own right. Its rich cultural heritage is showcased at Norwich Castle Museum, where it can also be found beautifully portrayed in the works of the Norwich School artists.

Nature abounds, with birdwatching at Titchwell and Strumpshaw Fen, home to bitterns, marsh harriers and the swallowtail butterfly, while seal colonies thrive on the coast at Blakeney and Horsey. Norfolk's cuisine reflects its rural and maritime legacy, with samphire scoured from the salt marshes, Cromer crabs, shrimps and oysters from the Wash, together with Norfolk Black Turkeys – the oldest turkey breed in the UK.

The county is learning to prosper in new ways to meet the needs of our changing world. In 2016 the United Kingdom voted to leave the European Union, yet the county of Norfolk is geographically well positioned to benefit from economic ties with countries across the North Sea and retains close links with Europe. Ironically, improving routes and communications facilitate quicker travel to Holland and Belgium than with much of England. Norfolk also maintains an important military role in the security of Great Britain. The airbase at RAF Marham is home to 617 'Dambusters' Squadron. In 2018 it was equipped with the new generation of F-35 Lightning fighter aircraft, already performing a major role in the safeguarding of Western Europe. The radar station at Neatishead has played an important role in the defence of the country since 1941 and today it is key to national and NATO air defences as part of the UK Air Surveillance and Control System (ASACS), in coordination with other sites across north Norfolk.

In the twenty-first century, Norfolk is looking outward and forward. Its improving communications link it to other parts of Britain and abroad, which will benefit the regional economy. It remains well placed, both geographically and in its outlook, to successfully embrace new challenges and to remain engaged in national developments and innovation, while managing to retain its special quality of life.

FURTHER READING

A list of titles for further reading is provided below. The very large range of publications available relating to Norfolk is extensive and it has been necessary to provide a selective range here, which will provide an introduction to most aspects. I have attempted to include the more readily accessible works, where possible.

Ashton, N., *Early Humans* (William Collins, 2017)

Ashwin T. and Davison, A., *An Historical Atlas of Norfolk* (Phillimore, 2005)

Ayers, B., *Norwich* (Batsford, 1994)

Ayers, B., *The German Ocean* (Equinox, 2016)

Bance, P., *Sovereign, Squire and Rebel: Maharajah Duleep Singh and the Heirs of a Lost Kingdom* (Coronet House, 2009)

Banger, J., *Norwich at War* (Wensum Books, 1974)

Barringer, C. (ed.), *Aspects of East Anglian Prehistory* (Geo Books, 1984)

Barringer, C. (ed.), *Norwich in the Nineteenth Century* (Gliddon Books, 1984)

Bond, R., Penn K. and Rogerson, A., *The North Folk; Angles, Saxons and Danes* (Poppyland, 1990)

Bottinelli, G. (ed.), *A Vision of England: Paintings of the Norwich School* (Norwich Castle Museum & Art Gallery, 2013)

Carew, T., *The Royal Norfolk Regiment* (Hamish Hamilton, 1967)

Champion, M., *Seahenge: A Contemporary Chronicle* (Barnwell, 2000)

Clabburn, P., *The Norwich Shawl* (HMSO, 1995)

Crosby, A., *A History of Thetford* (Phillimore, 1986)

Davies, J.A., *The Land of Boudica: Prehistoric and Roman Norfolk* (Heritage/Oxbow, 2009)

Davies, J.A. (ed.), *The Iron Age in Northern East Anglia: New Work in the Land of the Iceni* (BAR British Series 549, 2011)

Davies, J.A. and Pestell, T., *A History of Norfolk in 100 Objects* (The History Press, 2015)

Davies, J.A., Riley, A., Levesque, J.-M. and Lapiche, C. (eds), *Castles and the Anglo-Norman World* (Oxbow, 2016)

Davies, J. and Robinson, B., *Boudica: Her Life, Times and Legacy* (Poppyland, 2009)

Davison, A., *Norfolk Origins 5: Deserted Villages in Norfolk* (Poppyland, 1996)

Dymond, D., *The Norfolk Landscape* (The Alastair Press, 1990)

Edwards, N.G., *Ploughboy's Progress: The Life of Sir George Edwards* (Centre of East Anglian Studies, 1998)

Gilbert, G.F.A. and Osbourne, D.J., *Charles Burrell & Sons Ltd: Steam Engine Builders of Thetford* (Friends of the Charles Burrell Museum, 1991)

Haining, P. (ed.), *Norfolk Broads: The Golden Years. Pictures and Memories 1920s–1950s by Philippa Miller* (Halsgrove, 2008)

Hedges, A.A.C., *Yarmouth is an Antient Town* (Blackall Books, 1959)

Hoare, A., *An Unlikely Rebel: Robert Kett and the Norfolk Rising, 1549* (Wymondham Heritage Society, 1999)

Holmes, N., *The Lawless Coast* (Larks Press, 2008)

Hooton, J., *The Glaven Ports* (Jonathan Hooton, 1996)

McWilliam, N., Sekules, V. and Brandon-Jones, M., *Life and Landscape: P.H. Emerson: Art and Photography in East Anglia, 1885–1900* (Sainsbury Centre, 1986)

Malster, R., *The Norfolk & Suffolk Broads* (Phillimore, 2003)

Margeson, S., *The Vikings in Norfolk* (Norfolk Museums Service, 1997)

Margeson, S., Seillier, F. and Rogerson, A., *The Normans in Norfolk* (Norfolk Museums Service, 1994)

Margeson, S., Ayers, B. and Heywood, S. (eds), *A Festival of Norfolk Archaeology* (Norfolk & Norwich Archaeological Society, 1996)

Marsden, A., *17th Century Norfolk Tokens* (Norfolk Museums Service, 2018)

Meeres, F., *A History of Norwich* (Phillimore, 1998)

Meeres, F., *Norfolk in the First World War* (Phillimore, 2004)

Meeres, F., *Norfolk in the Second World War* (Phillimore, 2006)

Meeres, F., *A History of Great Yarmouth* (Phillimore, 2007)

Moore, A., *The Norwich School of Artists* (Norfolk Museums Service, 1985)

Moore, A.W., *Norfolk & The Grand Tour* (Norfolk Museums Service, 1985)

Pestell, T., *Viking East Anglia* (Norfolk Museums Service, 2019)

Pocock, T., *Norfolk* (Pimlico, 1995)

Ramirez, J., *Julian of Norwich* (SPCK, 2016)

Reynolds, D., *Rich Relations: The American Occupation of Britain 1942–1945* (Phoenix Press, 2000)

Richards, P., *King's Lynn* (Phillimore, 2006)

Sealey, P.R., *The Boudican Revolt Against Rome* (Shire, 1997)

Smith, G., *Norfolk Airfields in the Second World War* (Countryside Books, 1994)

Soros, S.W. and Arbuthnott, C., *Thomas Jeckyll: Architect and Designer, 1827–1881* (Yale University Press, 2003)

Storey, N.R., *The Little Book of Norfolk* (The History Press, 2011)

Sutherland J. and Canwell, D., *The Holy Boys* (Pen & Sword Military, 2010)

Wade-Martins, P., *A Life in Norfolk's Archaeology: 1950–2016* (Archaeopress, 2017)

Wade-Martins, S., *A History of Norfolk* (Phillimore, 1984)

Watson, C., *Seahenge: An Archaeological Conundrum* (English Heritage, 2005)

Williamson, T., *The Origins of Norfolk* (Manchester, 1993)

Williamson, T., *The Norfolk Broads: A Landscape History* (Manchester, 1997)

Williamson, T., *East Anglia* (English Heritage, 2006)

INDEX